VALUES CLARIFICATION

A Handbook of Practical Strategies
for Teachers and Students

REVISED EDITION

SIDNEY B. SIMON
LELAND W. HOWE
HOWARD KIRSCHENBAUM

A HART BOOK

A & W VISUAL LIBRARY • NEW YORK

This book is dedicated to Louis E. Raths. Without his inspiring and pioneering work in Values Clarification, this book could never have been written.

PUBLISHED BY
A & W PUBLISHERS, INC.
95 MADISON AVENUE
NEW YORK, NEW YORK 10016

LIBRARY OF CONGRESS CATALOG CARD NUMBER: 70-187023
ISBN: 0-89104-174-5

PRINTED AND BOUND IN CANADA

CONTENTS

PART ONE

PART TWO

VALUES CLARIFICATION
A Handbook of Practical Strategies
for Teachers and Students

PART ONE

THE VALUES-CLARIFICATION APPROACH

THE VALUES-CLARIFICATION APPROACH

Every day, every one of us meets life situations which call for thought, opinion-making, decision-making and action. Some of our experiences are familiar, some novel; some are casual, some of extreme importance. Everything we do, every decision we make and course of action we take, is based on our consciously or unconsciously held beliefs, attitudes and values.

Students, no less than adults, face problems and decisions every day of their lives. Students, too, ponder over what and how to think, believe, behave. So often what goes on in the classroom is irrelevant and remote from the real things that are going on in students' lives—their daily encounters with friends, with strangers, with peers, with authority figures; the social and academic tasks that assault or assuage their egos. Young people are being asked and are asking themselves important personal and theoretical questions that will lead them to important decisions and action.

Should Bill and I live together before marriage? Shouldn't we know if we're really compatible?

School seems so irrelevant. Why not drop out and get a better education on my own?

Do we have to take to the streets, maybe even violent-

ly, to bring about any political change these days?

How do I know whether marijuana is really harmful to me or not?

Does religion have some meaning in my life, or is it nothing more than a series of outmoded traditions and customs?

Do I care more about a girl's looks than about her personality?

What occupation shall I choose, so that I don't spend my life like so many others who despise the jobs they go to every morning?

Should I let my hair grow longer?

How can I really enjoy working and living, and avoid getting into the rat race for the convertible and the house in the suburbs?

What can I do to help improve race relations these days?

Why is it that at the end of every weekend I feel anxious and guilty about all I didn't do?

This is a confusing world to live in. At every turn we are forced to make choices about how to live our lives. Ideally, our choices will be made on the basis of the values we hold; but frequently, we are not clear about our own values.

Some typical areas where we may experience confusion

and conflict in values are:

politics	friends
religion	money
work	aging, death
leisure time	health
school	race
love, sex	war-peace
family	rules, authority
material possessions	
culture (art, music, literature)	
personal tastes (clothes, hair style, etc.)	

All of us, young or old, often become confused about our values. But for young people especially, the values conflicts are more acute.

The children and youth of today are confronted by many more choices than in previous generations. They are surrounded by a bewildering array of alternatives. Modern society has made them less provincial and more sophisticated, but the complexity of these times has made the act of choosing infinitely more difficult.

How then, does a young person learn how to direct his life through a world full of confusion and confict?

Traditionally, adults, motivated by a sincere desire to have the younger generation lead happy and productive lives, have guided them in the following ways:

1. Moralizing is the direct, although sometimes subtle, inculcation of the adults' values upon the young. The as-

sumption behind moralizing runs sometimes like this: My experience has taught me a certain set of values which I believe would be right for you. Therefore, to save you the pain of coming to these values on your own, and to avoid the risk of your choosing less desirable values, I will effectively transfer my own values to you.

One of the problems with this approach is that it is becoming increasingly less effective. The direct inculcation of values works when there is complete consistency about what constitutes "desirable" values. But consider the youth of today. Parents offer one set of shoulds and should nots. The church often suggests another. The peer group offers a third view of values. Hollywood and the popular magazines, a fourth. The first grade teacher, a fifth. The seventh grade teacher, a sixth. The President of the United States, a seventh. The spokesmen for the New Left and the counterculture, an eighth; and on and on.

Bombarded by all these influences, the young person is ultimately left to make his own choice about whose advice or values to follow. But young people brought up by moralizing adults are not prepared to make their own responsible choices. They have not learned a process for selecting the best and rejecting the worst elements contained in the various value systems which others have been urging them to follow. Thus, too often the important choices in life are made on the basis of peer pressure, unthinking submission to authority, or the power of propaganda.

Another problem with the direct inculcation of values is that often it results in a dichotomy between theory and practice; lip-service is paid to the values of the authority,

while behavior contradicts these values. Thus we have religious people who love their neighbors on the Sabbath
and spend the rest of the week competing with them. And
we have patriots who would deny freedom of speech to
any dissenters whose concept of patriotism is different
from theirs. And we have good students who sit quietly in
class and wouldn't dare speak without raising their hands,
but who freely interrupt their friends and parents in the
middle of a sentence. Moralizing so frequently influences
only people's words and little else in their lives.

2.   Some adults maintain a laissez-faire attitude toward the transmission of values. The rationale here is:
"No one value system is right for everyone. People have to
forge their own set of values. So I'll just let my children
or students do and think what they want without inter-
vening in any way; and eventually everything will turn
out all right."

The problem here is that everything doesn't usually
turn out all right. Young people, left on their own, experience a great deal of conflict and confusion. In our experience, most young people do not need adults running their
lives for them, but they do want and need help.

3.   Modeling is a third approach in transmitting values. The rationale here is: "I will present myself as an attractive model who lives by a certain set of values. The
young people with whom I come in contact will be duly
impressed by me and by my values, and will want to
adopt and emulate my attitudes and behavior."

This approach acknowledges two realities—first, the

importance of setting a living example for a learner to follow; and, second, the necessity in teaching values for the deeds to match the words.

However, the fact is that the young person is exposed to so many models to emulate. Parents, teachers, politicians, movie stars, friends, all present different models. How is the young person to sort out all the pros and cons and achieve his own values? When it comes time to choose an occupation, or a spouse, or a candidate, or to decide how far to go in the back seat of a car on a Saturday night date, how does the young person choose his own course of action from among the many models and many moralizing lectures with which he has been bombarded? Where does he learn whether he wants to stick to the old moral and ethical standards or try new ones? How does he develop his own sense of identity? How does he learn to relate to people whose values differ from his own?

4. The values-clarification approach tries to help young people answer some of these questions and build their own value system. It is not a new approach. There have always been parents, teachers, and other educators who have sought ways to help young people think through values issues for themselves. They have done this in many ways.

However, the values-clarification approach we are discussing in this book is more systematic and more widely applicable. It is based on the approach formulated by Louis Raths, who in turn built upon the thinking of John Dewey. Unlike other theoretical approaches to values, Raths is not concerned with the *content* of people's values, but the *process of valuing*. His focus is on how people come to hold certain beliefs and establish certain behavior patterns.

Valuing, according to Raths, is composed of seven sub-processes:[1]

PRIZING one's beliefs and behaviors
    1. prizing and cherishing
    2. publicly affirming, when appropriate

CHOOSING one's beliefs and behaviors
    3. choosing from alternatives
    4. choosing after consideration of consequences
    5. choosing freely

ACTING on one's beliefs
    6. acting
    7. acting with a pattern, consistency and repetition

Thus, the values-clarification approach does not aim to instill any particular set of values. Rather the goal of the values-clarification approach is to help students utilize the above seven processes of valuing in their own lives; to apply these valuing processes to already formed beliefs and behavior patterns and to those still emerging.

To accomplish this, the teacher uses approaches which help students become aware of the beliefs and behaviors they prize and would be willing to stand up for in and out of the classroom. He uses materials and methods

---

[1] Raths, Louis; Harmin Merrill; Simon Sidney: *Values and Teaching;* Charles E. Merrill, Columbus, Ohio, 1966.

which encourage students to consider alternative modes of thinking and acting. Students learn to weigh the pros and cons and the consequences of the various alternatives. The teacher also helps the students to consider whether their actions match their stated beliefs and if not, how to bring the two into closer harmony. Finally, he tries to give students options, in and out of class; for only when students begin to make their own choices and evaluate the actual consequences, do they develop their own values.

The growing amount of empirical research that has been done on the values-clarification approach, and the large amount of practical experience with this approach by thousands of teachers, indicate that students who have been exposed to this approach have become less apathetic, less flighty, less conforming as well as less over-dissenting. They are more zestful and energetic, more critical in their thinking, and are more likely to follow through on decisions. In the case of underachievers, values clarification has led to better success in school.[2]

This manual provides the teacher with 79 specific, practical strategies to help students build the seven valuing processes into their lives. Some teachers set aside a certain amount of time each day or each week for values clarification, much as some social studies teachers set aside a block of time each week for current events. This block of time can range from five minutes to an hour or more a day. In some schools, there are elective courses in

---

[2]Kirschenbaum, Howard: "Current Research in Value Clarification." Chapter in *Advanced Value Clarification*; University Associates, La Jolla, Cal., 1977.

values clarification, identified by many different titles.

Another approach to teaching values clarification is to incorporate it into standard subject matter. Most subject matter can be taught on any or all of the following levels: the facts, the concepts and the values level. For example, in teaching the Thanksgiving story on the facts level, the teacher might ask what date the Pilgrims landed on Plymouth Rock. On the concepts level, the class would discuss freedom of religion and emigration, perhaps making comparisons with other historical or contemporary events. On the values level, the teacher might ask the class questions like, "Is there anything you value so strongly that you would leave this country if it were taken away? If you had to cross the ocean and, like the Pilgrims, could take only one suitcase full of belongings, what do you prize so much that you would put it in that suitcase?"

Still another, and often the most sophisticated use of values clarification is to tie the values-clarification strategies in with subject matter and skill learning so as to advance both the search for knowledge and the search for values.[3] For example, an ecology unit in a science class might begin with several values-clarification strategies aimed at helping students identify their feelings and priorities about certain environmental issues. Then the class might study the related subject matter. They might then decide on a plan of action utilizing their new knowledge in a project aimed at improving the environment. Thus

---

[3]Harmin, Merrill; Kirschenbaum, Howard; Simon, Sidney: *Clarifying Values Through Subject Matter*; Winston Press, Minneapolis, 1973.

the students have engaged in the valuing processes of prizing, choosing and acting, and at the same time they have learned the subject matter of the course.[4]

[4]For a list of materials currently available and workshops offered in the values-clarification area, write to the National Humanistic Education Center, 110 Spring St., Saratoga Springs, New York, 12866.

HOW TO USE THIS BOOK

Most of the activities in this book have not appeared previously in print. Several of the strategies have been suggested by other teachers and group leaders, and it has usually been difficult, if not impossible, to identify the original source. Wherever a strategy has come to us from some source, we have done our best to give appropriate credit.

Many of the strategies—like the Fallout Shelter or the Alligator River Problem—are "one-time" strategies. That is, they would not ordinarily be repeated with the same group. Other strategies, like Rank Ordering and Interviewing, can be done repeatedly as long as new questions or items are used. For these repeatable strategies, we offer numerous examples to indicate the many variations that are possible. The teacher can choose items which best suit his purposes and can also create his own additional items.

Each strategy is described in a standard format. First comes the purpose, which always relates to one or more of the seven processes of valuing. Then the procedures are described in detail. Finally, there are notes and tips to the teacher, and additional suggestions if appropriate.

This structuring is done for the sake of clarity and easy reference only. There is no one right way to use these strategies. Change them! Adapt them! Think of your own examples!

The strategies are numbered consecutively in this book. However, this numbering is more or less arbitrary, and is chiefly useful for identification purposes. There is no hard and fast sequence which is recommended. A great deal depends on the age and needs and experience of the particular group. The teacher is free to pick and choose the strategies he would like to use, and he can decide for himself in which order he prefers to use them. Recommendations are made here and there about strategies which are good follow-up activities after other strategies. It is advisable that the teacher read through the whole book so that he can get a clear idea of the range of activities that are described here. He can then use them in the way that would be most appropriate for his group.

In this book strategies are discussed in the context of classroom use. However, most of them are very adaptable for use by parents and group leaders in other than classroom situations. In addition, almost all of these strategies can be applied to any age level, as long as the items are adapted to the specific group. To illustrate this point we have provided different examples for elementary, secondary and adult age levels for the Voting, Ranking and Interviewing strategies and the Alligator-River Problem.

Many of the strategies are equally effective when used with students individually, or in small groups, or with a whole class. Where one approach seems to be preferable to another, this is indicated in the text. However, the teacher is free to use the strategy as he sees fit.

The teacher will also have to determine how much time to spend on each strategy and on the discussion that follows a strategy. We prefer to leave this decision to the teacher, who knows the needs of his own group better than we possibly could. Needless to say, the teacher should plan the exercise beforehand, and estimate roughly how much time it will take.

We would like to alert the teacher to be on the lookout for the many ways that these strategies can be applied to the teaching of subject matter. For example, the teacher could ask a student to role-play a literary or historical character that the class is studying. Using the Public Interview Strategy (#12), the teacher interviews the student, who answers the questions as though he were the person being studied. After the interview, the student can answer the same questions all over again. This time he answers for himself instead of for the famous person. Other specific hints about classroom application are mentioned in the notes to the teacher at the end of each strategy.

When using the activities and strategies for values clarification, encourage a classroom atmosphere of openness, honesty, acceptance and respect. If students feel that something they say about their own beliefs and behavior is going to be ridiculed by their peers or frowned upon by the teacher, they will not want to share their thoughts and feelings about values issues.

The teacher must help the students learn to listen to one another. One of the best ways he can do this is to be a model of a good listener himself. He can indicate by his verbal and nonverbal expressions that he is interested in what the students think, and will seriously consider their ideas and possibly be influenced by them. (Teachers who think their students are too young and inexperienced to have developed worthwhile ideas should not use the values-clarification approach. Values imposition would probably be more their style; and they should be open about it and not hide behind values-clarification jargon and techniques.)

But even the best intentioned teachers sometimes find themselves moralizing. Watch the class. See if they seem to be telling you what they think you want to hear. Tell them not to hesitate to let you know if they feel pressured toward a certain point of view or set of values.

Whenever a student does not want to respond, he should always be given the right to pass. This is essential! The teacher should accept a pass just as he would any other response—with respect.

The teacher should participate in the exercises and discussions whenever possible. The best time for the teacher to give his view is toward the end, after the students have had a chance to think things through for themselves and to express their own points of view. The teacher should present himself as a person with values (and often with values confusion) of his own. Thus the teacher shares his values, but does not impose them. In this way, he presents the class with a model of an adult who prizes, chooses and acts according to the valuing process. The teacher gets a chance to share his actual values as does any other member of the class. The particular content of his values holds no more weight than would anyone else's; but his behavior reinforces the seven valuing processes.

We wish our readers success in the use of these strategies and welcome any suggestions, adaptations, or ideas for new strategies. We would like to encourage you to send your contributions to any of the authors, or to National Humanistic Education Center, 110 Spring St., Saratoga Springs, New York 12866. If we use any of your material in any further publications on the values-clarification approach, it will be faithfully acknowledged.

PART TWO

THE VALUES-CLARIFICATION STRATEGIES

STRATEGY NUMBER 1

Twenty Things You Love to Do

PURPOSE

An important question to ask in the search for values is, "Am I really getting what I want out of life?" A person who simply settles for whatever comes his way, rather than pursuing his own goals, is probably not living a life based upon his own freely chosen values. He usually ends up by feeling that his life is not very meaningful or satisfying. However, before we can go about building the good life, we must know what it is we value and want. This activity helps students examine their most prized and cherished activities.

PROCEDURE

The teacher passes out paper and asks the students to write the numbers from 1 to 20 down the middle of the sheet. He then says, "And now will you please make a list of 20 things in life that you love to do."

To encourage the students to start filling out their lists, he might add, "They can be big things in life or little things." He may offer an example or two of his own. Or he might suggest, "You might think in terms of the seasons of the year for things you love to do."

The teacher also draws up his own list of 20 items, and as he reaches the end of his list, he might tell his students that it is perfectly all right if they have more than 20 items, or fewer than 20 items on their lists.

When the lists are done, the teacher tells the students to use the left-hand side of their papers to code their lists in the following manner:

1. A dollar sign ($) is to be placed beside any item which costs more than $3 each time it is done. (The amount could vary, depending on the group.)

2. The letter *A* is to be placed beside those items the student really prefers to do *alone*; the letter *P* next to those activities he prefers to do with other *people*; and the letters *A-P* next to activities which he enjoys doing equally alone or with other people.

3. The letters *PL* are to be placed beside those items which require *planning*.

4. The coding *N5* is to be placed next to those items which would *not* have been listed *five* years ago.

5. The numbers *1* through *5* are to be placed beside the five most *important* items. The best loved activity should be numbered 1, the second best, 2, and so on.

6. The student is to indicate next to each activity *when* (day, date) it was last engaged in.

TO THE TEACHER

This strategy can be repeated several times throughout the year. It is a good idea to save the lists and compare them over a period of time.

Any more than five or six codings at one sitting generally overloads the circuits.

The teacher might see ways of making additional use of the lists. For example, he might ask his students to describe on paper or orally to a partner how they like to do the item they marked with the number 1. The student would tell with whom, at what time, under what circumstances, he likes to engage in the chosen activity.

Or the teacher might ask the student to choose one of the items on his list and then list privately, or discuss with a partner, five advantages, pleasures, gains, benefits, or satisfactions he gets from that activity.

A student might volunteer to write his list on the board, with the option to omit any items he'd rather not share. The teacher gives him a Public Interview based on his list. (See Strategy Number 12.)

I Learned Statements (Strategy Number 15) are an excellent follow-up to this strategy.

ADDITIONAL SUGGESTIONS

The teacher might want to add additional elements to the coding system suggested above. Here are some more suggestions that the teacher may use or adapt:

1. Use the letter *R* for those things on your list which have an element of RISK to them. It can be physical risk, emotional risk, or intellectual risk.

2. Put an *I* next to any item which involves INTIMACY.

3. Mark with an *S* any item which can only be done in one particular SEASON of the year.

4. Put the letters *IQ* next to any item which you think you would enjoy more if you were smarter.

5. Place the letter *U* next to any item you have listed that you think other people would tend to judge as UNCONVENTIONAL.

6. Put the letter *C* next to items which you think other people might judge as very CONVENTIONAL.

7. Use the code letters *MT* for items which you think you will want to devote increasingly MORE TIME to in the years to come.

8. Put the letters *CH* next to the things you have listed which you hope your own CHILDREN would have on their own lists someday.

9. Which items on your list do you feel nobody would conceivably REJECT you for loving? Code them with the letters *RE*.

10. Place the letter *O* next to any items you would

rather do OUTSIDE. Place the letters *IN* next to any items you would rather do INSIDE.

11. Put an *MI* by any of your items which you would not be. able to do if you moved 1,000 MILES south from where you now live.

12. Choose three items which you want to become really BETTER at doing. Put the letter *B* next to these items.

13. Which of the items that you put on your list would you want to see on a list made by the person you love the very most? Mark these items with an *L*.

14. Next to each item write the name of a person you want most to talk to about that specific item.

15. Write the letter *F* next to those items which you think will not appear on your list five years from now.

STRATEGY NUMBER 2

Values Grid

PURPOSE

The values grid usually drives home the point that few of our beliefs or actions fit all seven of the valuing processes. This activity indicates what steps we must take in order to develop stronger and clearer values.

PROCEDURE

The teacher either gives students, or asks them to construct, a "values grid," as shown below:

Issue	1	2	3	4	5	6	7
1							
2							
3							
4							
5							
Etc.							

Then the teacher and the students name some general issues, such as energy, water pollution, population control, abortion, race relations, a specific election, a school issue, etc. The students list these issues on the lines on the left-hand side of their papers. Next to each of these general issues the student is to write privately a few key words that summarize for him his position or stand on that issue.

The seven numbers heading the columns on the right-hand side of the paper represent the following seven questions:

1. Are you *proud* of (do you prize or cherish) your position?

2. Have you *publicly affirmed* your position?

3. Have you chosen your position from *alternatives*?

4. Have you chosen your position after *thoughtful consideration* of the pros and cons and consequences?

5. Have you chosen your position *freely*?

6. Have you *acted* on or done anything about your beliefs?

7. Have you acted with *repetition*, pattern or consistency on this issue?

The teacher can read these seven questions to the students, or write them on the board, or the students can write the key words (those that are underlined) at the top of each column. The students then answer each of these seven questions in relation to each issue. If they have a positive response to the question on top, they put a check in the appropriate box. If they cannot answer the question affirmatively, they leave the box blank.

TO THE TEACHER

After they have completed marking their grids, the students can form trios, with each student discussing one of the issues, his position on it, and how it did or didn't meet the seven valuing processes. Your students have undoubtedly engaged in many discussions of the issues they have listed in the values grid. It is worthwhile for the students to note how the approach here differs from discussions they may have had previously. It should become apparent that here they are not being called on to defend the content of their beliefs, but are rather being asked to evaluate how they arrived at their convictions and how firm they are in their beliefs.

The students should understand the seven processes, which are the basis for the values strategies they are doing. Many teachers post the seven processes permanently in the classroom.

The students might want to save their papers and look at them again at some future date. They will be able to see not only whether the content of their beliefs has undergone any change, but, more important, whether there have been any changes in the quality and degree of their convictions.

STRATEGY NUMBER 3

Values Voting

PURPOSE

Voting provides a simple and very rapid means by which every student in the class can make a public affirmation on a variety of values issues. It develops the realization that others often see issues quite differently than we ourselves do and legitimizes that important fact.

PROCEDURE

The teacher reads aloud one by one questions which begin with the words, "How many of you...?" For example, "How many of you like to go on long walks or hikes?" After each question is read the students take a position by a show of hands. Those who wish to answer in the affirmative raise their hands. Those who choose to answer negatively point their thumbs down. Those who are undecided fold their arms. And those who want to pass simply take no action at all. Discussion is tabled until the teacher has completed the entire list.

SAMPLE VOTING LIST

The following voting list is designed for use with secondary students. (Many more examples for use at various levels are suggested below.)

Preface each of the following questions with the statement, "How many of you. . . ."

1. think teenagers should be allowed to choose their own clothes?

2. would raise your children more strictly than you were raised?

3. watch TV more than three hours per day?

4. think the most qualified person usually wins in school elections?

5. think there are times when cheating is justified?

6. could tell someone they have bad breath?

7. think going steady is important in order to achieve social success?

8. regularly attend religious services and enjoy them?

TO THE TEACHER

Voting is an excellent way to introduce specific values issues into the classroom. For example, you might want to do a unit on race relations. A voting list made of questions about the students' feelings, thoughts and actions on race-related issues (e.g. How many of you. . . have ever visited in the home of a friend of a different race? Think that black people and white people are different beyond skin color?) provides an effective way to stimulate student interest in the unit.

Once students get the hang of voting, they can create excellent voting lists of their own. They can make up lists of questions about their own concerns and then conduct the voting themselves. We encourage this because it means the teacher will not be making all the decisions about which values issues will be discussed.

Voting lists should not be too long. They lose their effectiveness after about ten or more items. Discussion may or may not follow.

The teacher votes too. To keep from influencing the vote, the teacher holds his vote until a split second after most of the students have committed themselves to a position.

In some cases, the teacher might want to vary the voting procedure. For example, he might want to add the following statement to the voting directions, "On some issues you may have *very strong* feelings—for or against. If you have a very positive response to a question, you may show this by waving your raised hand. If you have a very negative response, you may choose to show this by pointing your thumb down."

Sometimes the teacher may ask if any student would care to choose one of the questions and discuss his reaction to it.

Voting is a very easy and useful feedback device and the teacher may use it to check on himself, as well as for value clarification. For example, "How many of you liked the story we just read?" or "How many of you need to hear the instructions one more time?"

ADDITIONAL SUGGESTIONS

We have provided many more examples of questions for values voting lists. The questions listed below are divided into four categories. The first listing is General and may be used for most ages, except the very youngest. The Secondary/Adult list is most appropriate for older adolescents and adults, although some of the questions may be used at younger levels. The Intermediate list is most suitable for pre- and early adolescents, although many of the questions are appropriate for older adolescents and adults as well. The Primary list is most appropriate for young children.

Many of the questions can be reworded and used in other values strategies. For example, by placing the words, "Have you ever...." or some other appropriate beginning in front of some of the items, the questions can be used with the Interviewing strategies.

Each of the questions below should be prefaced by the statement, "How many of you...." or "How many here...."

Examples for General Use with All Ages

1. ___ enjoy watching movies on TV?
2. ___ go to church or temple regularly?
3. ___ enjoy going to church or temple?

4. ___ think children should have to work for their allowance?

5. ___ have ever been in love?

6. ___ are in love right now?

7. ___ have ever felt lonely even in a crowd of people?

8. ___ have a close friend of another race?

9. ___ have had someone from another race to your house for dinner or to play?

10. ___ would like to bring in a voting list tomorrow?

11. ___ have learned something from a person eight years or younger in the past year?

12. ___ have a favorite hobby or pastime?

13. ___ feel that religion is an important part of your life?

14. ___ think students are losing respect for teachers?

15. ___ think you are racially prejudiced?

16. ___ think familiarity breeds contempt?

17. ___ wish you were home right now doing whatever you like to do?

18. ___ think that at this point in your life you are a complete flop or failure?

19. ___ think that we should have spent all that money to go to the moon?

20. ___ would like to go into politics some day?

21. ___ have ever personally witnessed race conflict?

22. ___ have ever participated in race conflict?

23. ___ have ever had problems so bad you wished you could die so you wouldn't have to face them?

24. ___ are in favor of having American police follow the example of the British "Bobbies"—no live ammunition?

25. ___ would live forever if you could?

26. ___ think more federal aid should be given to welfare programs?

27. ___ would want black students to come to an all-white social function?

28. ___ would want white students to come to an all-black school?

29. ___ think that women should stay home and be primarily wives and mothers? Men...husbands and fathers?

30. ___ think that most students feel free to talk with their parents?

31. ___ think most students feel free to talk with their teachers?

32. ___ find it difficult to listen to people sometimes?

33. ___ have a clear idea of your own values?

34. ___ have ever had a scary dream?

35. ___ have read a book just for fun in the last three weeks?

36. ___ play a musical instrument?

37. ___ enjoy going on a picnic?

38. ___ have ever daydreamed in class?

39. ___ have been hurt by a friend?

40. ___ are an only child?

41. ___ have/had a favorite game as a child?

42. ___ would favor a law to limit families to two children?

43. ___ often think of death?

44. ___ would like to make some changes in your life?

45. ___ have ever gone skiing?

46. ___ think there are times when cheating is justified?

47. ___ think it is all right for older brothers and sisters to discipline younger ones?

48. ___ would like to go to the moon someday?

49. ___ think that most people cheat on something?

50. ___ sometimes have secrets you don't even tell your best friends?

51. ___ would like to have a celebrity as a friend?

52. ___ would rather be older or younger than you are now?

53. ___ like to do things with your family?

54. ___ think most adults understand young people today?

55. ___ would like to be President? A senator? A Supreme Court judge?

56. ___ have ever been to Europe? To another state in the U.S.?

57. ___ have a special place of your own?

58. ___ have lived in the city all your life?

59. ___ would rather live someplace else?

60. ___ know someone who has fought in a war?

61. ___ have watched a sunrise with someone this past year? A sunset?

62. ___ have slept in a tent this year?

63. ___ wear seat belts when riding in a car?

64. ___ would be willing to donate your body to science when you die?

65. ___ think school attendance ought to be optional?

66. ___ enjoy giving gifts?

67. ___ would like to grow a beard or mustache?

68. ___ give money to at least one charity?

69. ___ like yogurt?

70. ___ would rather work alone?

71. ___ have written a letter to your Congressperson or the President?

72. ___ have ever been seriously burned?

73. ___ own a horse?

74. ___ would like to jump from a plane with a parachute?

75. ___ have had a snowball fight?

76. ___ enjoy family meals?

77. ___ think you will be only too happy to retire when the time comes?

78. ___ think the job of parenting should be shared by all adults?

79. ___ play sports with your family?

80. ___ get enough sleep at night?

81. ___ usually don't sleep very well at night? Have trouble going to sleep?

82. ___ enjoy taking walks?

83. ___ think there should be a law guaranteeing a minimum income?

84. ___ have difficulty sitting still for more than an hour?

85. ___ wouldn't mind having classes with no textbooks?

86. ___ enjoy playing a musical instrument?

87. ___ think teenagers should go steady?

88. ___ think that the way you view death is related to the way you view life?

89. ___ have ever visited someone in a hospital?

90. ___ would like to take karate lessons?

91. ___ think students should pay their own way through college?

92. ___ would like to own a sailboat?

93. ___ think that the father should have as much responsibility for parenting as the mother?

94. ___ think that communication is more open in families today?

95. ___ dream of owning a sports car?

96. ___ consciously try to save energy by turning your lights out when they're not needed?

97. ___ are happy in your work?

98. ___ would like your body to be cremated when you die?

99. ___ think capital punishment should be abolished?

100. ___ would like to retire at age 40? 50?

101. ___ think we should take more trips to the moon?

102. ___ could invite someone you couldn't stand to your home?

103. ___ are fully satisfied with what you have accomplished in life so far?

104. ___ would put $5,000 in the stock market if you had that much in savings?

105. ___ think we ought to legalize "pot" (marijuana)?

106. ___ approve of abortion?

107. ___ think we ought to have lowered the voting age?

108. ___ think we ought to have compulsory school attendance until age 16?

109. ___ think we ought to raise the voting age?

110. ___ think you are a well-organized person?

111. ___ know the contents of your top dresser drawer?

112. ___ would turn in a drug pusher to the law? If he/she were your friend?

113. ___ would turn in someone for using drugs? If he/she were your friend?

114. ___ have ever wanted to really hurt someone for something they did to you?

115. ___ have ever written a letter to the editor?

116. ___ have ever written a "dear John" letter? Received one?

117. ___ have ever been in a dramatic or comic play?

118. ___ think it is all right for men to wear wigs?

119. ___ used to be hall monitors in elementary school?

120. ___ spend less than $25 total for Christmas presents?

121. ___ have more than five pairs of shoes?

122. ___ think that teachers shouldn't say "hell" or "damn" in the classroom?

123. ___ have full polio protection?

124. ___ like to read the comics first thing in the Sunday paper?

125. ___ belong to a Christmas savings club?

126. ___ make some of the gifts you give at Christmas?

127. ___ have not been invited to a party you wanted to go to?

128. ___ feel that all of your family members feel they are a part of decision-making in the home?

129. ___ didn't have any cavities the last time you went to the dentist?

130. ___ have ever signed a petition?

131. ___ have ever broken an arm or leg?

132. ___ have not yet made plans for the coming summer?

133. ___ have ever caught a mouse in a mouse trap?

134. ___ are willing to admit when you are wrong?

135. ___ spend most of your time out-of-doors in nice weather?

136. ___ have hurt feelings when you are criticized?

137. ___ don't like to show that you're angry?

For Use with Secondary Students and with Adults

1. ___ feel that the feminist movement has had a mostly positive influence?

2. ___ think giving grades in school inhibits meaningful learning?

3. ___ approve of premarital sex for boys?

4. ___ approve of premarital sex for girls?

5. ___ would prefer a girl or a boy to marry someone from his or her own race?

6. ___ think sex education should be taught in the schools?

7. ___ think sex education instruction in the schools should include techniques for lovemaking, contraception?

8. ___ think today's kids are more courageous, adventurous, wise, involved, and concerned with life than the previous generations?

9. ___ think that teachers should discuss their personal lives with students?

10. ___ have recently begun a family tradition?

11. ___ think school administrators should be selected from the teaching staff on a rotating basis?

12. ___ think merit pay is a good thing?

13. ___ would approve of a marriage between homosexuals being sanctioned by priest, minister or rabbi?

14. ___ would approve of a young couple trying out marriage by living together for six months before actually getting married?

15. ___ have worked together as a family on a social issue?

16. ___ think that children ought to compete in school to prepare them for the "real" world after graduation?

17. ___ think that most schools today are exciting places?

18. ___ think that this school is an exciting place for students?

19. ___ think that most students have a clear idea of their values in life?

20. ___ think that the curriculum in most schools is designed for teachers rather than students?

21. ___ have a part-time job?

22. ___ would like teachers to be called by their first names?

23. ___ would like to change your profession/college/major/occupation if you had a chance?

24. ___ like to spend time with children?

25. ___ would encourage legal abortion for an unwed daughter?

26. ___ have spoken with homosexuals about their life style?

27. ___ would change to a job you really didn't like if it offered $10,000 a year more than you now make?

28. ___ think it's fun to learn new things?

29. ___ keep a compost pile?

30. ___ meditate?

31. ___ watch your weight?

32. ___ approve of people marrying as young as possible?

33. ___ think that schools do not prepare young people well enough for life?

34. ___ think that teachers should transmit their own values to students?

35. ___ would take your children to religious services even if they didn't want to go?

36. ___ think you would change your life style if your income were doubled?

37. ___ would actively participate in a fair-housing movement in your community if someone got the ball started?

38. ___ would approve of contract marriages in which the marriage would come up for renewal every few years?

39. ___ would be upset if your daughter were living with a man who had no intentions of marriage? If your son were living with a woman, etc.?

40. ___ enjoy smoking?

41. ___ would be upset if organized religion disappeared?

42. ___ think the government should help support day-care centers for working mothers?

43. ___ think that parents should be subsidized to pick any school they want for their children?

44. ___ think grades (marking) ought to be abolished in school?

45. ___ would be in favor of a "halfway house" for drug addicts in your neighborhood?

46. ___ think that the role of paraprofessionals in medicine should be expanded?

47. ___ think there is nothing morally wrong with using the pill for birth control?

48. ___ watch the checker in the supermarket to see if he cheats you?

49. ___ would not hesitate to marry someone from a different religion? From another race? Ethnic group?

50. ___ have ever participated in a demonstration? Carried a picket sign?

51. ___ ride your bike to work/school?

52. ___ would approve of another adult reprimanding

your child for using abusive language?

53. ___ think it's okay to dye your hair a different color?

54. ___ expect to get a doctorate someday?

55. ___ own a credit card?

56. ___ have purchased a hardbound book which was not a text in the past year?

57. ___ have grown up on a farm?

58. ___ want to give or receive an engagement ring? Want it to be a diamond?

59. ___ subscribe to a magazine?

60. ___ collect savings stamps? Actually paste and trade them in?

61. ___ have ever taken a sex education course?

62. ___ have ever sent in money to a TV telethon?

63. ___ think that the young people of today are spoiled?

64. ___ give money to a beggar?

65. ___ pick up hitchhikers?

66. ___ have ever tended a garden?

67. ___ will never spank your children?

68. ___ frequently burn candles at home?

69. ___ would approve of a couple using artificial insemination if the husband were sterile?

70. ___ watch the Super Bowl every year?

71. ___ keep a journal or diary?

72. ___ would like to take up glider soaring?

73. ___ think we should legalize mercy killings?

For Use in the Intermediate Grades

1. ___ dream about being famous?

2. ___ have ever cheated on an exam?

3. ___ jog regularly?

4. ___ have ever wished you were a child again?

5. ___ would smoke a marijuana cigarette if it were offered to you?

6. ___ would love to direct a large symphony orchestra someday?

7. ___ have ever finished a piece of furniture?

8. ___ would stay at a party where marijuana was being smoked?

9. ___ have a poster on a wall at home?

10. ___ think your teachers are not strict enough?

11. ___ would go to school if you didn't have to?

12. ___ almost never fight with your brothers and sisters?

13. ___ would like to change something about this school?

14. ___ would like to earn some money?

15. ___ would like to be a marine someday?

16. ___ answer the phone differently sometimes just for fun?

17. ___ use an alarm clock to wake up in the morning?

18. ___ would like to ride a motorcycle?

19. ___ don't like to talk in class?

20. ___ would mind if your teacher were a sloppy dresser?

21. ___ have bought something in a store and asked not to receive the paper bag?

22. ___ plan on going to college?

23. ___ have a brother or sister in college?

24. ___ have a TV set in your bedroom?

25. ___ would like to be voted best liked in the class?

26. ___ have a clothing allowance and are allowed to purchase your own clothes?

27. ___ have your own bedroom?

28. ___ would like to have the same teacher(s) next year?

29. ___ enjoy blizzards?

30. ___ subscribe to a magazine which comes addressed to you?

31. ___ have ever visited your father's place of work? Your mother's?

32. ___ got something for Christmas that was advertised on TV?

33. ___ have a best friend of the opposite sex?

34. ___ would like to be a member of the safety patrol?

35. ___ would like to call your teacher by his/her first name?

36. ___ would like to live in another country?

37. ___ would like to stay on a deserted island by yourself for a week?

38. ___ have read a children's book with a young person in the past week?

39. ___ think that girls and boys should be in separate classrooms?

40. ___ would like to change your hair style?

41. ___ would ask your parents to stop smoking?

42. ___ do some kind of volunteer work?

43. ___ have ever been a scout?

44. ___ know someone who has been very sick or has died from drugs?

45. ___ know what you would like to do when you finish school?

Examples for Use in the Primary Grades

1. ___ have a pet at home?

2. ___ have a favorite movie star?

3. ___ would like to live on a farm?

4. ___ would like to live in a different city someday?

5. ___ like chocolate ice cream?

6. ___ like asparagus?

7. ___ think school is fun?

8. ___ have a favorite TV show?

9. ___ wish you could stay up later at night?

10. ___ like to go on long car trips?

11. ___ have a best friend?

12. ___ would rather play in a baseball game than watch one?

13. ___ have ever climbed a mountain?

14. ___ daydream sometimes?

15. ___ think you will smoke cigarettes someday?

16. ___ have been to the movies in the past two weeks?

17. ___ would rather go to the movies than to school?

18. ___ like to be teased?

19. ___ sometimes tease others?

20. ___ receive an allowance?

21. ___ have to work for your allowance?

22. ___ would like to change your name?

23. ___ would like to have an important job someday?

24. ___ can swim?

25. ___ would like your parents to have a baby?

26. ___ go to Sunday School or religious class?

27. ___ would like to go to Disneyland?

28. ___ think teachers should be allowed to spank you?

29. ___ have a private place to go when you want to be alone?

30. ___ have a friend or relative in a foreign country?

31. ___ like to sing to yourself?

32. ___ watch Sesame Street?

33. ___ are afraid of the dark? Earthquakes? Your teacher?

34. ___ are members of a Brownie Troop or Cub Pack?

35. ___ like frozen custard better than regular ice cream?

36. ___ think that it is all right for girls to play with Hot Wheels?

37. ___ think that it is all right for boys to play with Barbie dolls?

STRATEGY NUMBER 4

Rank Order

PURPOSE

Each day of our lives we must make choices between competing alternatives. Some of them are minor decisions: "Shall I stay home tonight and watch TV or go to a friend's house for the evening? Shall I wear my blue or my white sweater?" And some are major decisions: "Shall I buy a car or save my money for college?" "Shall I go to school this summer or work?"

This strategy gives students practice in choosing from among alternatives and in publicly affirming and explaining or defending their choices. It demonstrates simply and clearly that many issues require more thoughtful consideration than we tend to give them.

PROCEDURE

The teacher explains to the class that he is going to ask them some questions which will require them to look deeper into themselves and make value judgments. He will give them three (or four) alternative choices for responding to each question and ask them to rank order these choices according to their own value-laden preferences.

The teacher then reads a question, writes the choices on the board and calls upon six to eight students in turn to give their rankings. Each student quickly gives his first, second and third rankings. Of course, students may say, "I pass." After six to eight students have responded to a question, the teacher may give his own rankings. Then a class discussion may follow, with students explaining their reasons for their choices, even if they weren't among the original six to eight to speak.

SAMPLE RANK-ORDER QUESTIONS

The following rank-order questions were developed for use with secondary students. Additional rank orders for other age levels are given below:

1. Where would you rather be on a Saturday afternoon?

   _____ at the beach

   _____ in the woods

   _____ in a discount store

2. How do you learn best?

   _____ through lectures

   _____ through independent study

   _____ through seminars

3. Which would you rather be?

   _____ an American Negro

   _____ an African Negro

   _____ a European Negro

4.   Which would you give the lowest priority to today?

_____ space

_____ poverty

_____ defense

_____ ecology

TO THE TEACHER

Be sure to have students rank all the alternatives, not just their first choices. Try to have them name their choices instead of saying "2-3-1," or the like; and discourage them from saying, "The same" when their response is identical to the previous student's. Renaming the choices helps everyone consider the alternatives more carefully.

Sometimes students may want to add alternatives to the choices offered by the teacher. After the initial ranking is completed, the teacher may say, "It's possible that many of you have other ideas that don't appear here that you would include if you had made up this rank order. Are there any other alternatives you'd like to add to our list? How would you rank them?"

The rank-order strategy can be used in a number of ways. The teacher or students can put one or two rank-order questions on the blackboard each day. Students may think about and discuss them whenever they have time.

The teacher may make up several rank-order questions related to the lesson for the day. They may be used as lead-ins to create interest and spark discussion, as midway activities to summarize and give new life to the lesson, or as closing activities to give the students something to mull over after the class. For example, in a class which was getting ready to look at the rise of the civil rights movement, the teacher started with this rank-order question:

Which death do you consider the greatest loss?

> Martin Luther King's
> John F. Kennedy's
> Malcolm X's

Or the teacher may give students several rank-order questions during the last five minutes of the class when their attention has begun to wander. It is very likely that they will find themselves wanting to stay beyond the bell.

Students may be asked to make up rank-order questions based on their own concerns. They will most likely pose questions that you might never have thought to ask.

Sometimes the teacher will create a rank-order question spontaneously when a class discussion on some issue raises several alternatives.

Additional Suggestions

Below are more examples of rank-order questions to be used at the various levels.

For General Use

1.   Which is most important in a friendship?
         _____ loyalty
         _____ generosity
         _____ honesty

2. Which season do you like best
   _____ winter
   _____ summer
   _____ spring
   _____ fall

3. If I gave you $500, what would you do with it?
   _____ save it
   _____ give it to charity
   _____ buy something for myself

4. Which do you think is most harmful?
   _____ cigarettes
   _____ marijuana
   _____ alcohol

5. How late should 14-years-olds be allowed to stay out on a weekend night?
   _____ 10 P.M.
   _____ 12 P.M.
   _____ it's up to them

6. If you were a parent, how late would you let *your* 14-year-old stay out?
   _____ 10 P.M.
   _____ 12 P.M.
   _____ it's up to him/her

7. Where would you rather live?
   _____ on a farm
   _____ in the suburbs
   _____ in an inner city

8.   Which do you like best?

_____ winter in the mountains

_____ summer by the sea

_____ autumn in the country

9.   Which would you rather be?

_____ an only child

_____ the youngest child

_____ the oldest child

10.   Which pet would you rather have?

_____ a cat

_____ a dog

_____ a turtle

_____ a parakeet

11.   If you were President, which would you give the highest priority?

_____ space program

_____ poverty program

_____ defense program

12.   Which would you *least* like to be?

_____ very poor

_____ very sickly

_____ disfigured

13. Whom would you prefer to marry? A person with
        _____ intelligence
        _____ personality
        _____ sex appeal

14. Which do you think more money should be spent on?
        _____ moon shots
        _____ slum clearance
        _____ cure for cancer

15. What would you be most likely to do about a person who has bad breath?
        _____ directly tell him
        _____ send him an anonymous note
        _____ nothing

16. Which would you rather have happen to you if you had bad breath?
        _____ be told directly
        _____ receive an anonymous note
        _____ not be told

17. When you worry about your mark on an exam do you think about
        _____ yourself?
        _____ your parents?
        _____ pleasing the teacher?
        _____ getting into college?

18. Which type of teacher do you most prefer?

_____ strict in the classroom but little homework

_____ strict in the classroom and much homework

_____ easy-going in the classroom but much homework

19. Which would you least like to do?

_____ listen to a Beethoven symphony

_____ watch a debate

_____ watch a play

20. Which would you most like to improve?

_____ your looks

_____ the way you use your time

_____ your social life

21. How do you have the most fun?

_____ alone

_____ with a large group

_____ with a few friends

22. If you had $500 to spend on decorating a room, would you spend

_____ $200 for an original painting, the rest on furniture?

_____ $400 on furniture and $100 for an original painting?

_____ entire sum on furniture?

23. Pretend you are married and have your own family. Your mother has died and your father is old. What would you do?

_____ invite him to live in your home

_____ place him in a home for the aged

_____ get him an apartment for himself

24. Which would you rather your sister gave you for your birthday?

_____ $5 to buy yourself something

_____ a $5 gift of her choice

_____ something she made for you

25. If someone's parents were in constant conflict, which would be better for them to do?

_____ get divorced, and the father leave home

_____ stay together and hide their feelings for the sake of the children

_____ get divorced, and the children live with their father

26. What would you do for your parents' anniversary?

_____ buy them a nice present

_____ make them a big party

_____ take them out to dinner and a show

27. If you had two hours to spend with a friend, which would you do?

_____ stand on a corner

_____ go to a movie

_____ go for a walk

_____ go bowling

28. You've spent a great deal of time picking a gift for a friend. You give it to him personally. What would you rather have him do if he doesn't like the gift?

_____ keep the gift and thank you politely

_____ tell you he doesn't like it

_____ return the gift to the store without telling you

29. If you were a pacifist and you found out your friend supports certain wars, would you

_____ discontinue the relationship?

_____ overlook the discrepancy in views?

_____ try to change his viewpoint?

30. Which would you rather do?

_____ hike up a mountain with a good trail but difficult grade

_____ blaze a new trail through the woods

_____ hike on a fairly level, well-marked trail

31. Which of the following measures should be taken to alleviate the population problem?

_____ keep abortion legal

_____ limit each family to two children and sterilize the parents afterwards

_____ distribute birth control information everywhere

_____ trust people's common sense to limit the size of their families

32. Imagine you are living with a family of a different religion for a few months. At meals they say a grace which is affiliated with a religion different from yours. Would you

_____ join in

_____ sit silently

_____ try to get them to change the grace to a more universal one

33. What would you think if you saw a man burning a dollar bill?

_____ that the man is foolish

_____ that the man has integrity

_____ why doesn't the man give that dollar to me?

34. If you suddenly inherited money and became a millionaire, would you

     _____ share your wealth through charities, educational trust funds, etc.?

     _____ continue in your present job and activities?

     _____ really live it up?

35. If you had $10 you didn't need for something else, would you

     _____ get a newspaper subscription?

     _____ buy another shirt or blouse?

     _____ treat a friend to dinner?

36. You are well off financially and you inherit $10,000. What would you do?

     _____ put it in a savings bank

     _____ invest it all in the stock market

     _____ spend it all

37. Which would be your job preference?

     _____ hard and dirty work at $80 per week

     _____ clean and easy work at $40 per week

     _____ dirty but easy work at $60 per week

38. Which do you most want money for?

_____ to buy your own food & clothing

_____ to go places on your own

_____ to feel independent

39. Where would you seek help in a strange city?

_____ a church

_____ a police station

_____ a people's community center

40. Which would you find easiest to do

_____ campaign for contributions to a Thanksgiving food drive

_____ tutor other students

_____ be a hospital volunteer worker

41. Which would you be most willing to do?

_____ install a solar heating system?

_____ turn down the thermostat to 65° and wear sweaters?

_____ move to a warmer climate?

42. Which would you be least willing to do?

_____ join a picket line

_____ take part in a sit-in

_____ sign a petition

43. In your leisure time, what would you most like to do?

_____ weave, make pottery, or do some craft

_____ play a guitar

_____ water ski

44. What is the most serious problem in this city today?

      _____ discrimination in jobs and housing

      _____ transportation

      _____ hunger

      _____ overcrowding

45. What is the most serious domestic issue in the United States today?

      _____ crime prevention

      _____ welfare

      _____ inflation

46. Which would you most like to be?

      _____ owner of a small business

      _____ employee in a large corporation

      _____ employee in a small business

47. Which would you most like to see?

      _____ integration of races

      _____ separate nations for different races

      _____ separate areas within existing communities for each race and/or nationality

48. Which would you least like to be?

      _____ a rifleman firing point-blank at the charging enemy

      _____ a bomber on a plane dropping napalm on an enemy village

      _____ a helicopter pilot directing a naval bombardment of enemy troops

49. Where would you most like to visit?

_____ England

_____ Russia

_____ China

50. Which would you prefer?

_____ a short, exciting life with a peaceful death

_____ a long, dull life with a peaceful death

_____ a long, exciting life with a painful death

51. Which do you like to do most?

_____ play tennis

_____ play football

_____ swim

52. Which would you like to do most?

_____ learn to skin dive

_____ learn to ride a mini-bike

_____ learn to ride a horse

53. Which would you like to do most?

_____ travel by automobile

_____ travel by bus

_____ travel by airplane

_____ travel by train

54. Which would you like to do most?

_____ learn to fly an airplane

_____ learn to drive a car

_____ learn to ride a motorcycle

55.   Which would you like to do most?
_____ shoot a high-powered rifle
_____ shoot a shotgun
_____ shoot arrows
_____ not shoot at all

56.   Which would you like to do most?
_____ become a jet fighter pilot
_____ become an astronaut
_____ become a surgeon

57.   Which do you like most?
_____ math
_____ English
_____ social studies

58.   Which do you like best?
_____ Jello
_____ pie
_____ ice cream

59.   Which would you prefer to be?
_____ a prison guard
_____ a garbage collector
_____ an assembly-line worker

60.   Which would you least like to do?
_____ be a hangman
_____ be a member of a firing squad
_____ be an executioner in a peniten-
          tiary

61. Whom do you like least?

    _____ a shoplifter

    _____ a drug pusher

    _____ a confidence man

62. What is the most serious problem in your school?

    _____ apathy

    _____ drugs

    _____ discipline

63. Which would you be most willing to do?

    _____ serve in the armed forces

    _____ serve in the Peace Corps

    _____ work in an urban ghetto

64. In which of these situations would you be most likely to take some action?

    _____ a car is parked with its headlights on in broad daylight

    _____ a dog has scared a kitten up a telephone pole

    _____ some big boys are trying to tie tin cans to the tail of a dog.

65. How would you spend an inheritance?

    _____ on travel

    _____ on education

    _____ on entertainment

66. Which would you least like to be?

    _____ deaf

    _____ an amputee

    _____ blind

67. What would you most like to do with your friends during your leisure time?

    _____ play a sport or game

    _____ go to the movies or watch TV

    _____ just talk

    _____ play cards

For Use with Secondary Students and Adults

1. If you were with your family in a boat that capsized far from shore and there was only one life preserver would you

    _____ save your wife/husband?

    _____ save one of your children?

    _____ save yourself?

2. If you were stranded on a deserted island which would you rather have with you?

    _____ the Bible

    _____ the complete works of Shakespeare

    _____ the history of civilization

3. Which of these would be most difficult for you to accept?

    _____ the death of a parent

    _____ the death of a spouse

    _____ your own death

4. How would you break off a three-year relationship with someone you've been dating steadily?

    _____ by telephone

    _____ by mail

    _____ in person

5. Which of these jobs would you like most?

    _____ schoolteacher on an Indian reservation

    _____ director of an inner city project

    _____ coordinator of social action projects for a liberal suburban church

6. What is the worst thing you could find out about your teenager? (Does the sex make any difference?)

    _____ that he has been shoplifting

    _____ that he is a high school dropout

    _____ that he is promiscuous

7. Which would you be more concerned about as you grow older?

    _____ lung cancer

    _____ overweight

    _____ declining vision

8. Would you rather be a teacher in a classroom that was

    _____ teacher centered?

    _____ student centered?

    _____ subject-matter centered?

9. As a small child, which did you like least?

    _____ recess

    _____ show and tell

    _____ storytime

10. Which would you prefer to give up if you had to?

    _____ economic freedom

    _____ religious freedom

    _____ political freedom

11. If you needed help in your studies, whom would you probably go to?

    _____ your friend

    _____ your teacher

    _____ your parent

12. Which of these problems do you think is the greatest threat in the nearest future?

    _____ overpopulation

    _____ too much leisure time

    _____ water and air pollution

    _____ crime

13. During a campus protest where would you be most likely to be found?

    _____ in the midst of it

    _____ gaping at it from across the street

    _____ in the library minding your own business

14. Which would you rather see a cutback of federal expenditures for?

_____ urban research

_____ educational allotments

_____ foreign aid

15. During what period in U.S. history do you think you would have been a most effective leader?

_____ colonization of America

_____ Civil War

_____ the Industrial Revolution

16. How would you rather spend a Saturday evening?

_____ at a good play

_____ at a good concert

_____ at a good movie

17. How would you rather spend a Friday evening?

_____ at a nightclub

_____ at home alone

_____ at a party at a friend's home

18. Which would you least like your son or daughter to do?

_____ marry out of necessity

_____ marry outside of his/her race

_____ smoke marijuana once a week

19. If you were about to be drafted into the army which would you do?

_____ go willingly

_____ leave the country

_____ go to jail

20. Which is the most beautiful sight to you?

_____ a sunset

_____ a person giving blood

_____ a baby taking his/her first step

21. Which do you like least?

_____ an uptight indoctrinator

_____ a cynical debunker

_____ a dull, boring fact giver

22. Which would you most like to take a course in?

_____ sex education

_____ race relations

_____ ecology

23. Which would you first join?

_____ a woman's/man's consciousness-raising group

_____ an environmental action group

_____ a community food cooperative

24. Which of these people would you have the most trouble introducing to your friends?

_____ a racially mixed couple

_____ Christine Jorgenson

_____ the Grand Dragon of the Ku Klux Klan

25.   Which best describes the way you handle money?

_____ spend freely

_____ always look for bargains

_____ budget carefully

26.   If one of your friends and your spouse were attracted to each other which would you prefer?

_____ for them to be open about their relationship

_____ for no one to know

_____ for them to keep it a secret from you alone

27.   Which would you want most in a best friend?

_____ someone who will tell you that your fianceé isn't good enough for you

_____ someone who will listen to your problems

_____ someone who is aware of other people's needs

28.   Your friend has written a book which you think is lousy. If he asks for your opinion what would you tell him?

_____ the whole truth

_____ as much as you think he can stand

_____ what he wants to hear

29. *Men.* What kind of wife would bother you most?

    _____ one who interrupts her husband

    _____ one who spends too much money

    _____ one who keeps a messy house

30. *Women.* What kind of husband would bother you most?

    _____ one who interrupts his wife

    _____ one who spends too much money

    _____ one who keeps a messy house

31. *Teenagers.* Which do you think is the worst?

    _____ to become (or get someone) pregnant (unwed)

    _____ to be dependent upon hard drugs

    _____ to date someone from another race

For Use in the Intermediate and Primary Grades

1. Which kind of teacher would you prefer?

    _____ a nasty person but a good teacher

    _____ a nice person but a poor teacher

    _____ personality and teaching ability about average

2.   Which do you like least?

_____ a classmate who plays practical jokes on you

_____ a classmate who constantly tattles

_____ a classmate who gossips about other people

3.   What kind of present would you like most to get?

_____ a surprise present

_____ a present you already know about

_____ a present you pick out

4.   To whom would you tell a secret?

_____ your friend

_____ your teacher

_____ your parent

5.   What would you consider the worst experience?

_____ telling on a best friend

_____ changing schools

_____ getting lost in a shopping center

6.   Where would you most like to go?

_____ to the zoo

_____ to the planetarium

_____ to a horror movie

_____ to the library

7. Which would you most like to have?

   _____ one best friend

   _____ many friends

   _____ two or three good friends

8. Which would be easiest for you to do with your older brother or sister?

   _____ borrow money from him/her

   _____ go out with him/her

   _____ talk to him/her about a problem

9. What should an allowance be used for?

   _____ saving for something you want

   _____ spending on whatever you want at the moment

   _____ buying presents for others

10. What would you do if you saw your best friend steal some candy from a store?

   _____ report him

   _____ pretend you didn't see

   _____ ask him to share it with you

11. Which do you like best for dessert?

   _____ cake

   _____ pie

   _____ fruit salad

   _____ ice cream

12. Which would you rather do on a Saturday morning?

   _____ sleep late

   _____ play with a friend

   _____ watch TV

13.   Which would you least like to do?

_____ move to a new school

_____ lose your wallet

_____ break a leg

14.   Which would you rather be?

_____ a fireman/woman

_____ a policeman/woman

_____ a mailman/woman

15.   Which of these would you most like to have as your neighbor?

_____ a boy or girl three years younger than you who owns a pony

_____ a family with a swimming pool

_____ a new boy or girl your age

16.   Which of these would you most like to see in your neighborhood?

_____ a house being painted

_____ a house being torn down

_____ a house being built

17.   Which of these would you most like to see in your nieghborhood?

_____ ice cream wagon

_____ a parade

_____ a bookmobile

18.   Which of these would you want most as a neighbor?

_____ a teacher

_____ a circus clown

_____ a dentist

19. Which of these would you want most as a neighbor?

_____ a boy your age

_____ a girl your age

_____ a teenager

20. Which of these would you want most as a neighbor?

_____ a young blind person

_____ a young crippled person

_____ an old person

21. Which would make you most uneasy?

_____ a thunderstorm

_____ a new babysitter

_____ going to bed alone in the dark

22. With whom would you rather spend your vacation?

_____ a friend

_____ a teacher

_____ your family

23. Which do you least like to do?

_____ get up in the morning

_____ go to bed at night

_____ keep your room neat

_____ take naps

24. Which do you like best in school?

_____ reading

_____ arithmetic

_____ spelling

25. Which would you prefer to do?

_____ do better in reading

_____ make a new friend

_____ go on a long vacation

26. Which do you like best in school?

_____ art

_____ music

_____ gym

27. If you had to go on a long trip, how would you rather travel?

_____ by train

_____ by plane

_____ by ship

28. Which chore would you rather do?

_____ wash dishes

_____ dust the furniture

_____ take the garbage out

29. Which would you rather play?

_____ piano

_____ drums

_____ violin

30. What would you do if someone hit you?

_____ tell the teacher

_____ hit him/her back

_____ walk away

31.   Which would be hardest for you to do?

     _____ show a bad paper to your parents

     _____ walk away from a fight

     _____ wait your turn when you have something exciting to say

32.   Which would be hardest for you to do?

     _____ move to a new school

     _____ meet a new person

     _____ dance with a girl/boy

33.   Which would you least like to do?

     _____ go to a birthday party without a gift

     _____ go to a Halloween party without a costume

     _____ go to a party with a torn dress/trousers

34.   Which would you least like to do?

     _____ go into a dark room

     _____ slide down a very high slide

     _____ ride a bicycle on a busy street

35.   When playing house, would you rather be the

     _____ mother

     _____ father

     _____ baby

36.   Where would you like to spend your vacation?

     _____ at the shore

     _____ in the mountains

     _____ at your grandparents' house

37.   Which would you rather be?

_____ a kitten

_____ a kangaroo

_____ a lion

38.   Which would you rather do?

_____ play in the snow

_____ swim in a pool

_____ swim in the ocean

39.   What kind of person do you least like to sit next to? Someone who

_____ talks a lot

_____ looks at your paper

_____ can't sit still

40.   What would you do if a bully bothered you on your way home from school?

_____ tell your parents

_____ tell him you are not afraid of him

_____ take a different way home

41.   Which animal would you like to be?

_____ tiger

_____ monkey

_____ snake

42.   How would you rather have your parent punish you?

_____ by spanking you

_____ by taking away your favorite game or toy

_____ by talking to you

43.   Which would you rather explore?

_____ a tree

_____ a mountain

_____ a river

44.   Which would you hate most?

_____ getting a spanking

_____ going to the doctor for a shot

_____ losing a $5 bill

45.   What would you least like to do?

_____ sit near someone who looks dirty

_____ sit near someone who talks a lot

_____ sit near someone who teases you

46.   How would you spend $5?

_____ buy a game

_____ go to the movies

_____ treat the gang

47.   Which is the most difficult for you to do?

_____ eat something you really dislike

_____ do a report

_____ clean up your bedroom

48.   Which school job do you like best?

_____ being a messenger

_____ cleaning blackboards

_____ being desk inspector

49.   Where would you prefer to sit?

_____ near the window

_____ near the door

_____ in the front of the room

50.   Which would be hardest for you?

_____ to admit you told a lie

_____ to tell someone you broke his window

_____ to admit you cheated

51.   What do you like to do best?

_____ play games

_____ read a book

_____ play outside

52.   What would you do if someone took your favorite toy?

_____ hit him

_____ yell at him

_____ nothing

53.   Which color do you like best?

_____ red

_____ green

_____ blue

54.   With whom would you like most to play?

_____ with a boy

_____ with a girl

_____ alone

55. What is hardest for you to do?

      _____ be quiet

      _____ talk in front of the group

      _____ talk to the teacher

56. Which animal would you prefer to be?

      _____ an ant

      _____ a beaver

      _____ a donkey

57. If you were in an accident, which injury would upset you most?

      _____ two broken legs

      _____ temporary loss of hearing

      _____ temporary loss of eyesight

58. If you could be any person, who would you be?

      _____ President of the U.S.

      _____ top athlete in the country

      _____ most popular movie star in the country

59. If you were to be born with a great gift, which would you prefer?

      _____ a beautiful singing voice

      _____ great artistic ability

      _____ skill with your hands

60. What makes you happiest?

      _____ getting all A's and B's on your report card

      _____ taking a special trip with the gang

      _____ having a week off from school

61.   What makes you most angry?

_____ a teacher who treats you without respect

_____ a friend who won't listen to your side of an argument

_____ a brother/sister that tattles on you continuously

62.   Which is most important?

_____ to work hard for your future

_____ to love others

_____ to really know yourself

63.   Which would you prefer to have?

_____ $1,000

_____ a girl-/boyfriend who loves you

_____ a well paid, prestige position

64.   Which is worst?

_____ to be punished by teacher

_____ to have friends make fun of you

_____ to get bad grades on your report card

65.   Which would you prefer to marry?

_____ a rich person

_____ a happy person

_____ a famous person

66. Which song do you like best? (Teachers write in the choices.)

    _____   _____

    _____   _____

    _____   _____

67. Which picture makes you happiest?

    _____   _____

    _____   _____

    _____   _____

68. Which story do you like best?

    _____   _____

    _____   _____

    _____   _____

STRATEGY NUMBER 5

Either/or Forced Choice

PURPOSE

This exercise compels students to make a decision between two competing alternatives. "What characteristics do I identify with more—this or that?" In making their choices students have to examine their feelings and their self-concepts and values.

PROCEDURE

The teacher asks students to move the desks so that there is a wide path from one side of the room to the other. Then, the teacher asks an either/or question, like: "Which do you identify with more, a Volkswagen or a Cadillac?" By pointing or by actually posting the choice words on the two sides of the room he indicates that those who identify more with Volkswagens are to go to the one side and those who identify more with Cadillacs are to go to the other. Each student then find a partner on the side he has chosen and discusses with him the reasons for his choices. Discussion should be limited to two minutes.

Everyone returns to the center of the room. Then the

teacher gives another either/or forced choice, and the students again choose between the two alternatives by moving to the appropriate side of the room.

This may be repeated with five or six questions. The students should be instructed to find a new partner each time.

SAMPLE EITHER/OR CHOICES

Are you

_____ 1.   More of a saver or a spender?

_____ 2.   More like New York City or Colorado?

_____ 3.   More of a loner or a grouper?

_____ 4.   More like a rose or a daisy?

_____ 5.   More like breakfast or dinner?

_____ 6.   More like summer or winter?

TO THE TEACHER

This is an excellent introductory exercise for a new group.

ADDITIONAL EXAMPLES

Are you

_____ 1.   More like a teacher or a student?

_____ 2.   More yes or no?

_____ 3.   More here or there?

_____ 4.   More political or apolitical?

_____ 5.   More religious or irreligious?

_____ 6. More like the country or the city?

_____ 7. More like the present or the future?

_____ 8. More of a leader or a follower?

_____ 9. More physical or mental?

_____ 10. More of an arguer or an agree-er?

_____ 11. More intuitive or rational?

_____ 12. More establishment or antiestablishment?

_____ 13. More like a tortoise or a hare?

_____ 14. More likely to walk on thin ice or to tiptoe through the tulips?

_____ 15. More like patent leather or suede?

_____ 16. More like a paddle or a ping-pong ball?

_____ 17. More like an electric typewriter or a quill pen?

_____ 18. More like a falling star or a beacon light on a mountain?

_____ 19. More like a rock band or a baroque string quartet?

_____ 20. More like a clothesline or a kite string?

_____ 21. More like a "No Trespassing" sign or a "Public Fishing" sign?

_____ 22. More like a flyswatter or flypaper?

_____ 23. More like a roller skate or a pogo stick?

_____ 24. More like a file cabinet or a liquor chest?

_____ 25. More like a motorcycle or a tandem bicycle?

_____ 26. More like a gourmet or a MacDonald's fan?

_____ 27. More like a bubbling brook or a placid lake?

_____ 28. More like a screened porch or a picture window?

_____ 29. More like a mountain or a valley?

_____ 30. More like "A stitch in time" or "Better late than never?"

STRATEGY NUMBER 6

Forced-Choice Ladder

PURPOSE

The Forced-Choice Ladder serves the same purpose as the Rank-Order Strategy (Number 4) in that students must make choices from among competing alternatives. However, it is a much more complex strategy, with many more items. It requires considerable thought in weighing the relative importance of alternatives and their consequences. This strategy is also a sure-fire way of getting a group immersed in a heated, though usually friendly, discussion on issues and values.

PROCEDURE

The teacher gives students or asks them to construct a "forced-choice ladder," with 8 to 16 steps, depending upon how many items the teacher is going to present. (See figure below.)

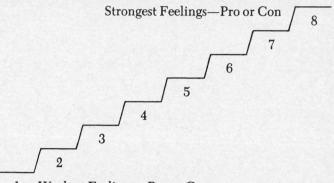

Strongest Feelings—Pro or Con

8

7

6

5

4

3

2

1   Weakest Feelings—Pro or Con

Then the teacher presents a series of statements, situations, or alternatives which call for value judgments by the students. Following the reading of each item the student is to write key words from the item on one of the steps of the ladder according to the strength of his feelings, pro or con, about that item. Explain to students that the ladder measures the intensity of their feelings only. It does not matter for this exercise whether the feelings are for or against. What matters is how strong the feelings are.

Sample items for a 12-step Forced-Choice Ladder are given below.

Students may cross out, draw arrows, or make changes as new items are presented. At the end, they have a few minutes to make their final arrangements.

After all the items have been read by the teacher and ranked by the students, the students are divided into small groups of three or four to compare and discuss their responses.

SAMPLE FORCED-CHOICE QUESTIONS

1.   George is a man who is constantly stressing law and order. He is concerned about the violence and law-breaking going on in our society. George is a building contractor. Frequently, when he gets parking tickets for his dump trucks he has them "fixed." Occasionally he does special favors for the building inspectors who inspect his work. (Key words: Law and order)

The teacher explains, "Think about how strongly you feel pro or con, about George in this situation, and put the words 'Law and Order' on one of the steps of the ladder. Don't put the items you feel positively about toward one end and the ones that generate negative feelings toward the other. In this exercise you are to rank the items according to the strength of your feelings, regardless of whether they are positive or negative."

2.   A woman believes that environmental awareness is crucial in the development of young minds. She often brings young people into the woods to experience nature. Along the way, she litters the trail with cigarette butts and an occasional soda pop can tab. (Environmental activist)

3.   A high school home economics teacher is considered

by everyone to be a fine teacher. She is trusted by the students. They can always turn to her. She knows that some of her students are engaging in premarital sex. She is concerned about this and gets prescriptions for birth control pills for some of her students. (Home ec teacher)

4.   A high school coach is constantly scolding his gym classes because they do not exercise enough. Yet, he parks his car as close as possible to the school so that he doesn't have to walk far. (The coach)

5.   A man who has two children is very much concerned about the population explosion. His wife wants more children, but he doesn't. He goes to the doctor and has a vasectomy without consulting his wife. (Population explosion)

6.   This man talks a great deal about how important it is for children to have a healthy emotional development. He seems to be permissive in his attitude toward children. One day he comes home and finds his three-year-old son playing with his genitals. He scolds the boy and hands him a large ball to play with instead. (Concerned father)

7.   A woman believes that we should have complete freedom of personal choice. She feels that she should be able to swim where she pleases and with whom she pleases. She builds a pool and operates a segregated swim club that keeps out blacks. (Swim club)

8.   A man cheats on his income tax each year, but donates all the money he saves by doing this to his

church. This money is in addition to his regular contributions. (Income tax)

9. A woman was very upset about the commercialization of Christmas. She tried to convince all the aunts and uncles to agree not to send Christmas gifts to their nieces and nephews. (Worried aunt)

10. An elementary school teacher sets high standards for her pupils' performance. Many of her students place very high on national tests. Most parents want their children to be in her class. The problem is she uses fear to motivate the students, and every morning about three or four of her students feel sick to their stomachs and do not wish to go to school. (High standards)

11. A blue-collar worker's son comes home from college and criticizes his father for working in a factory that is supplying metal parts for nuclear missiles and submarines. The father tells his son to shut up and points out that the money he earns in that factory is sending the punk through college. (Blue-collar worker)

12. A boy has graduated from high school and is going off to college. Before he leaves, his mother asks him to promise not to get involved in any political marches, protests, demonstrations, or to sign any petitions because anything like that could hurt his chances in the future. She reminds him that she and his father have made great sacrifices for him and they love him a great deal. (Protective mother)

TO THE TEACHER

We have found it to be more effective to present the statements, situations or stories verbally, one at a time, rather than dittoing them and presenting them to the students all at once.

An interesting and graphic extension of the forced-choice game is to have the students stand on a ladder marked on the floor to show where they have ranked certain items. This should be done after the usual procedure of ranking individually has been completed. For this purpose the ladder may be drawn with chalk, or the teacher may place sheets of $8\frac{1}{2} \times 11$ paper numbered consecutively, on the floor. The teacher will then call out the key words of the items, one by one, and the students will go and stand on the number corresponding to where they placed the item on their own papers. The students literally see where others stand on each issue.

ADDITIONAL SUGGESTIONS

1. A young boy tries to get even with the neighborhood grouch. On Halloween he fills a quart milk bottle with urine and leans it, without a lid, against her door. He rings the doorbell and runs. When she opens the door the urine goes all over her wall-to-wall carpet. (Halloween prank)

2. The neighborhood grouch wants to get even with the prankster. She has prepared one apple with a nail in

it. She plans to give it to the boy who ruined her carpet. (Neighborhood grouch)

3.   A man reports his neighbor to the Internal Revenue Service because he heard him mention at a party that he put something over on the government on his income tax. (Income tax)

4.   A vice-principal of a junior high school is very strict about the dress code. Any girl who comes to school in a very short dress must kneel before him. If her skirt does not touch the ground, she must go home immediately and change to more appropriate clothes. (Vice-principal)

5.   A college student is selling pot in the local high school to pay for his tuition. (Pot pusher)

6.   A junior high school student uses a knife to scare elementary school children into paying him protection money. (Shakedown)

7.   A woman comes out to her car in winter just after an ice storm. The windows are all covered with ice. She clears a tiny hole in the windshield and drives off. (Ice storm)

8.   An elementary school teacher is very strict about students running in the halls. During every break he goes into the teachers' room for a cigarette. (Halls)

9.   Two men get their kicks on Saturday night by going down to Greenwich Village and harassing homosexuals. (Greenwich Village)

10.   A big industrialist tells his plant manager to ar-

range it so their smokestacks don't pollute during the day. "Save it up and let it out only at night until this ecology stuff dies down." (Pollution)

11.   A Little League coach teaches his charges how to cheat without getting caught by the referee. (Coach)

12.   A man lets himself get talked into buying a vinyl hard-topped convertible. He then has to get air conditioning because the black top makes the car unbearably hot, and then he must get a bigger engine in order to run the air conditioner. (New car)

VARIATIONS

It is possible sometimes to change the basis for evaluation by changing the ratings at the two ends of the ladder. For the following items, the top of the ladder should be marked: "The person I'd most like to be like," and the bottom of the ladder: "The person I'd least like to be like." Students rank the items accordingly.

1.   A rich man who gives generously to all causes, including the Nazi Party. (Charity)

2.   A star athlete, always the first to come for practice and the last to leave. Some people worry that she may burn herself out young. (Athlete)

3.   A teacher who is friendly with all his students. He dresses like them and goes out socially with them. (Friendly)

4.   A woman with steady, directed determination be-

gins a new career, making constructive changes in her family and society. (Career woman)

5.   An ecologist who won't let his family use any paper products. (Paper)

6.   A devoted husband who sends flowers on all anniversaries and birthdays and never expects any presents himself. (Flowers)

7.   A college student who lends his tuition money to a friend who has to obtain an abortion. (Abortion)

8.   A student who witnessed a friend taking money from another friend's wallet, tells neither friend, but replaces the money himself. (Wallet)

9.   Parents who run their family with complete democracy—one person, one vote. Even the three-year-old has a vote on where to go for their vacation. (Vote)

10.   A white couple who, instead of having their own babies, adopt two black babies. (Babies)

11.   A cop who turns her own son in for smoking pot. (Incorruptible)

12.   A student who is very popular because he makes everyone feel good. He never expresses his own feelings or opinions if they are controversial. (Popular)

13.   A pilot has to make a forced landing and crashes into the woods instead of coming down on the elementary school playground because she saw two kids playing. (Airplane)

14.   A teacher who always looks the other way when kids cheat on tests he is proctoring. (Tests)

15.   A mother who has only one dress of her own because all her money goes for her three daughters to dress as knockouts in high school. (Dress)

16.   A junior high kid who cooks dinner two nights a week for two old invalids in his apartment building. (Cook)

* * *

For the forced-choice ladder items which follow, the top of the ladder should be marked: "Most objectionable classmate," and the bottom of the ladder: "Least objectionable classmate."[3]

1.   *Bother Bug*—Constantly interrupts the class by talking to the teacher and bothering other children.

2.   *Back Talker*—Talks back to his mother.

3.   *Cheater*—Cheats in a game.

4.   *Litterbug*—Drops trash on the sidewalk.

5.   *Borrower*—Borrows a pencil and does not return it.

6.   *Bully*—Beats up a younger child.

7.   *Shoplifter*—Steals candy from a store.

---

[3]This set of items, as well as the next two, are from the work of Richard Davis, principal of English Manor Elementary School, Rockville, Maryland.

8. *Firebug*—Sets fire to a building.

9. *Smoker*—Smokes cigarettes.

10. *Ratter*—Rats on a friend.

11. *Chewer*—Puts gum on the seat of a chair.

12. *Vandalizer*—Deliberately throws rocks through windows in the school.

In the next set of items for a forced-choice ladder, the student has to consider and rate how strongly he feels about issues of national concern today. He is to mark the top of the ladder: "Strongest feelings—pro or con," and the bottom of the ladder: "Weakest feelings—pro or con."

1. *Protest*—Violent protest as a method of bringing about change.

2. *Modify*—Modifying school curriculum to make it more relevant to the present society.

3. *Programs*—Greater community involvement in school programs.

4. *Drugs*—Developing programs in schools to combat drug abuse.

5. *Equality*—Men and women have similar opportunities for education and employment.

6. *Finance*—Greater federal financing for education.

7. *Politics*—Greater emphasis on selecting desirable nominees for high political positions.

8. *Law*—Laws, such as "no knock," that infringe on personal rights.

9. *Control*—National control to reduce pollution and protect natural resources.

10. *Sex*—Non-marital sex as a way of life.

11. *Teaching*—Improving teaching techniques to emphasize humanistic values.

12. *Model*—Adult education. aimed at providing a better adult model for youth.

13. *National*—A national curriculum which all children would learn.

14. *Religion*—Making religious programs more relevant to everyday life.

15. *Guardsmen*—Using National Guardsmen to control college student confrontations.

16. *Dollar*—The declining value of the dollar.

For the following forced-choice ladder the students are to rank each item according to: Strongest feelings—pro or con; weakest feelings—pro or con.

1. *Counterspy*—A person who accepts a government job to kill a person who is also in espionage.

2. *Doctor*—A doctor who prescribes name-brand drugs of a company in which he has been given stock by the salesman.

3. *Gambler*—A parent who plays the horses and neglects the needs of the family.

4. *Sex*—A person who satisfies his/her sex needs without marriage.

5. *Competitor*—A person who always plays to win.

6. *Fraud*—The president of a firm that purchases spoiled or poor cuts of meat to be sold to poor, unsuspecting, poorly educated people.

7. *Hit-Run Driver*—A driver who is going very fast to get to a business appointment. A child darts out between cars and is hit. The driver panics and keeps on going, leaving the injured child lying in the street.

8. *Gossip*—A person who just can't keep a confidence. Often spreads malicious, false information.

9. *Cheat*—The manager tells the checker in a supermarket to overcharge each customer two cents per item to make up for the shoplifting and food eating that goes on in the store.

10. *National Guardsman*—On guard duty at a college campus a National Guardsman is attacked by students and shoots at them.

11. *Two-Faced*—A person who talks about how great integration is, but wouldn't want to live next door to a black.

12. *Feminist*—A woman who believes strongly in gain-

ing equal power and recognition—always pays her own way when with a man.

13. *Hard Hat*—A person who uses an axe handle and fists to knock some sense into the heads of political demonstrators.

14. *Informant*—A neighbor who calls the police because she suspects the teenager across the street is using pot.

15. *Prankster*—A practical joker who ridicules people's weaknesses.

16. *Withdrawer*—A person who witnesses a violent crime, but doesn't want to get involved.

STRATEGY NUMBER 7

Values Geography[4]

PURPOSE

Values Geography can be used for several purposes. It is a good warm-up strategy to help students get better acquainted. Or it can be used on a deeper level, with older students, to help them recognize and clarify such life decisions as: "Where do I want to live?" "What kind of environment do I need?" Etc. Variations can help younger students respond to similar values questions. Finally, the strategy can be used to help make geography lessons come alive in the classroom.

PROCEDURE

The teacher asks students to move to the center of the classroom and imagine that the classroom represents a map of the U.S.A. (city, world, etc.—see variations). He then asks them a series of "values-geography questions." Following each question, the students are to move to a

---

[4]This strategy replaces the Value Survey of previous editions of *Values Clarification*.

location on the "map." For example, the teacher might ask, "Where were you born?" Students who were born in the midwest would move to the center of the classroom, and so on. There, they are instructed to find partners and to share for two minutes something about why they are there.

The teacher might then ask some clarifying questions, such as:

What are your feelings about being born there?

Are you proud to be associated with that part of the country?

What was the nicest thing about the place?

Is that a place where you would like to have your children be born and raised?

Then the teacher asks another question, like the ones below. Again, students move to that part of the map, find partners, and discuss why they are there.

SAMPLE VALUES GEOGRAPHY QUESTIONS

1.   Where is a place you would like to vacation for a week? (What would you do there? Etc.)

2.   Where is a place you would like to live for a year?

3.   Where would you least like to live or visit?

4.   (For adults) If you had to choose a place to retire, and money were no problem, where would you go?

5. Where would you choose to go to college?

6. Where is a place that something important in your life happened?

7. Where is a place, more than 100 miles away, that a special friend or relative lives? (What's special about that person?)

8. Where is the most beautiful place?

9. Where is a place you had a religious experience?

10. Where did you have one of your most important learning experiences?

Any number of new questions can be created and substituted for these.

VARIATIONS

Younger children may not have had the travel experience or the geographical perspective to enable them to become involved in a map of an entire country. In that case, it helps to reduce the scope of the map. For example:

1. Turn the floor of the classroom into a map of the city or town. Show them where some landmarks are—the schools, the river, downtown, etc.

2. Diagram the school.

3. For older students, the scale can be expanded—

Europe, Asia, Western or Eastern Hemisphere, the world, etc.

4. Physical maps can be created by placing strips of masking tape on the floor to represent the borders of countries, states, etc. This can help students learn to visualize maps, compare the relative size of states, and so on.

5. Students can be given a dittoed map of the U.S.A., city, world, etc., and be asked to code the map to indicate, for instance, where they were born, by placing the word "born" on the map. Each question would have a key word to be written on the students' maps—"vacation," "live," "retire," and so on.

6. The map can be drawn on the chalkboard, and students can respond by placing their initials on the map.

7. Other subject-oriented questions could be asked: Write the world "War" on your map, on the location which you think is most likely to experience such a conflict this year.

Where did you favorite novel take place? Write the title on that location on the map.

And so on.

STRATEGY NUMBER 8

Values Continuum

PURPOSE

The values continuum serves to open up the range of alternatives possible on any given issue. Students begin to realize that on most issues there are many shades of gray, and they are more likely to move away from the either/or, black/white thinking which often occurs when controversial issues are discussed in the classroom. The continuum also encourages students to make public affirmations of their opinions and beliefs.

PROCEDURE

An issue is identified by either the teacher or the class. This issue may have presented itself during a class discussion, or it may have been prepared beforehand by the teacher. We will use as an example the issue of government economic controls—often thought of as socialism vs. capitalism. (Additional examples for all age levels are given below).

The teacher draws a long line on the board, and he, or

he and the class, determine two polar positions on the issue. For example, one end position might be: "Complete
government control over economic affairs," and the other
end position might be: "Absolutely no government control
over the economic system." The two positions are placed
on the opposite ends of the line, as shown below.

Complete   No
control   :   :   :   :   :   :   control

The teacher then marks a series of points along the continuum, saying, "Between these end points there are numerous other positions. I am going to whip around the
room and ask you to tell me where *you* stand on this issue. Briefly describe your position, without giving your
reasons for holding that position. Tell me how much control you think is desirable and indicate where along the
continuum you want to place yourself. Later you can
share your reasons for your position. You may pass if you
wish."

The teacher goes around the room or calls on volunteers. The students place their names on the line and
briefly tell what their placement stands for. If five to ten
students respond, this is usually enough to get a spread of
opinion and to give everyone time to determine his own
position. The teacher may then put his own name on the
line and explain what his position is, or he, too, may pass.

By now every student in the room has considered the issue for himself, and free-wheeling discussion easily begins.

TO THE TEACHER

Sometimes the students tend to cluster together—because of peer pressure, fear of being different, laziness about considering the issues, coincidence, or because it was simply an unimaginative continuum. If clustering occurs students may be asked to write their answers on pieces of paper and the teacher can randomly choose some of these responses and post their positions on the continuum. Students must be allowed to write, "I pass," on their slips of paper. If clustering still tends to occur examine your continuum; it just may not be thought-provoking enough for your particular group.

Sometimes students (and adults) tend toward compulsive moderation in taking positions publicly. They place themselves right in the middle, thereby hoping to avoid conflict or the need to think critically. One thing the teacher can do if this occurs frequently is to simply eliminate the middle of the continuum. Explain that it's rare in life to be exactly in the middle of an issue.

The teacher must be particularly careful not to influence his students' choices. He must not verbally or nonverbally reward or praise students who have placed themselves on the continuum in positions he approves of. A wide spread of opinion usually means the continuum has encouraged good thinking about the issue.

VARIATIONS

The continuum can be a real or an imaginary line right down the center of the classroom. The students can actually place themselves on the line and negotiate with the people to their right and left to ascertain the correctness of their position. Students who are at the two opposite ends might profit from discussing their differences.

Or, the teacher can post a very long continuum on the wall, identifying the issue and the end positions. A marking pen and masking tape are made available. Students write in their names somewhere along the line whenever they wish. During the course of the week, as they see the continuum develop and have time to reflect on their choice, they may want to change their position. All they have to do is put masking tape over their name and write it in again at a new position. The same procedure can be followed now and then with new issues.

* * *

Additional suggestions—values continuum strategy:

1. What should the U.S. attitude be on involvement with other countries?

HELP EVERY COUN-						HELP NO COUNTRY
TRY EVEN IF NOT						—COMPLETE
ASKED TO DO SO	:	:	:	:	:	: ISOLATION

2. How far would you go to be popular with your group?

DO ANYTHING, IN-						DO NOTHING
CLUDING RISKING						AT ALL
SAFETY	:	:	:	:	:	:

3.   How much personal freedom do you have?

ALL DECISIONS ARE MADE FOR YOU	:	:	:	:	:	: COMPLETE FREE- DOM TO CHOOSE FOR YOURSELF

4.   How much freedom do you want?

ALL DECISIONS TO BE MADE FOR YOU	:	:	:	:	:	: COMPLETE FREE- DOM TO CHOOSE FOR YOURSELF

5.   How active are you in generating school spirit?

EARMUFF EDDIE	:	:	:	:	:	: CHEERLEADER CHARLENE

(Earmuff Eddie has so little school spirit that if he is forced to go to a pep assembly or game, he wears earmuffs and blinders and sits on his hands. Cheerleader Charlene gets so carried away with keeping the student body whipped into a frenzy that she doesn't know which team is winning and sometimes cheers when the other team makes a point.)

6.   How do you feel about what you wear?

HOLEY HAROLD— HAROLD ALWAYS HAS HOLES IN HIS CLOTHES EVEN WHEN THEY'RE NEW	:	:	:	:	:	: WRINKLE-FREE WALT—WALT IS SO METICULOUS HE EVEN IRONS HIS UNDERWEAR CAREFULLY

7.   How do you feel about fighting?

JET-FLIGHT JERRY—	:	:	:	:	:	: SCARFACE STU—
JERRY TAKES OFF						JUST LOOK AT STU
AT THE SIGN OF						CROSSWISE AND
ANY DISPUTE						YOU'LL FIND HIS
IN THE OPPOSITE						FIST IN YOUR FACE
DIRECTION						

8.   How are you at decisions?

COMPLETELY UN-	:	:	:	:	:	: DON'T WASTE A
ABLE TO MAKE						SECOND THINKING;
DECISIONS, EVEN						MAKE LIGHTNING-
ABOUT WHAT						FAST DECISIONS
TO WEAR						ABOUT EVERYTHING

9.   How do you feel about competition?

AVOID ANY SITUA-						WILL TRAMPLE
TION WHERE THERE	:	:	:	:	:	: ANYONE FOR THE
IS A CHANCE TO						CHANCE TO WIN,
WIN OR LOSE						AND USE ANY
						MEANS

10.   How much do you want from the family?

COMPLETE DEPEN-						COMPLETE INDIF-
DENCE ON FAMILY;	:	:	:	:	:	: FERENCE TO FAMI-
NO OUTSIDE INTER-						LY; WOULD RATHER
ESTS, FRIENDS, ETC.						BE RID OF THEM

11.   How do you feel about school?

DYNAMITE DAN—	:	:	:	:	:	: STOWAWAY STEVE—
STUDENTS WOULD						LOVES SCHOOL SO
BE BETTER OFF						MUCH THE JANITOR
IF THE SCHOOL						HAS TO DRIVE HIM
WERE BLOWN						OUT OF THE
TO BITS						SCHOOL EACH
						NIGHT BEFORE
						LOCKING UP

12. How much do you talk to other people?

TIGHT-LIPPED   :   :   :   :   :   : BLABBER-MOUTH
TIMMY   BERTHA

13. What will you eat?

PICKY PAUL   :   :   :   :   :   : EAT-ANYTHING-
                                          AND-EVERYTHING
                                          ELOISE

14. How do you feel about divorce?

STEADFAST STEL-   :   :   :   :   :   : MULTI-MARRYING
LA—UNDER NO CIR-   MARTHA—AT THE
CUMSTANCES   DROP OF THE FIRST
                                          UNKIND WORD

15. What do you do with your money?

HOARDING HAN-   :   :   :   :   :   : HANDOUT HELEN—
NAH—WON'T   SPENDS IT ALL OR
SPEND A PENNY   GIVES IT ALL
                                          AWAY. NEVER HAS
                                          ENOUGH LEFT FOR
                                          NECESSITIES

16. How do you feel about integration?

:   :   :   :   :   :   :   :   :   :   :   :   :
FAVORS COMPLETE   COMPULSIVE MODER-   ACTIVELY OPPOSED
AND IMMEDIATE   ATE FIGHTS FOR OPEN   WITHDRAWS CHILD
INTEGRATION.   HOUSING EXCEPT IN   FROM PUBLIC
ENFORCED BUS-   HIS OWN NEIGH-   SCHOOL
SING   BORHOOD

17. How do you like teachers to relate to you?

:   :   :   :   :   :   :   :   :   :   :   :   :
SUPER-BUDDY—   COMPULSIVE MODER-   VERY STRICT AND
LETS US DO   ATE YELLS CON-   PUNITIVE. BEATS
ANYTHING   STANTLY, BUT   US FOR A GRAM-
                  DOESN'T DO ANY-   MAR ERROR
                  THING TO STOP US

18.   How do you feel about defense?

:   :   :   :   :   :   :   :   :   :   :

PACIFIST PETE—
WANTS NO MILI-
TARY INSTALLA-
TIONS OR WEAPONS
DEVELOPMENT

NUCLEAR NED—
WANTS TO SPEND
ALL TAX MONEY
ON MAKING MORE-
POWERFUL BOMBS

19.   What percentage of the time are you happy?

SAD-SACK SARA   0 : : : : 100 HAPPY-TIME HELEN

20.   How do you feel about your school work?

WORRYWART   : : : : : : COULDN'T CARE
WILMA   LESS CAROL

21.   How much do you try to please the teacher?

REBEL RALPH   : : : : : : APPLE POLISHER AL

22.   How do you feel about teacher and pupil appear-
       ance?

INSPECTOR IRWIN— : : : : : : INDIFFERENT IGOR
INSPECTS TEACHERS'   —WOULD BARELY
AND STUDENTS'   BLINK AN EYELASH
FINGERNAILS EVERY   IF STUDENTS OR
MORNING   TEACHERS WORE
                                    SEE-THROUGH
                                    CLOTHES

23.   How clean do you keep your room?

EAT-OFF-THE-FLOOR : : : : : : GARBAGE-DUMP
ELLEN   GRETA

24.   How do you feel about premarital sex?

VIRGINAL   WILD-OATS
VIRGINIA—WEARS   : : : : : : WINNIE—
WHITE GLOVES ON   NEVER PASSES UP
EVERY DATE   AN OPPORTUNITY

25. How would you raise your child?

| SUPER-PERMISSIVE | | | | | | | SUPER-STRICT |
| PERRY | : | : | : | : | : | : | STEVE |

26. How do you feel about conservation?

WILDERNESS							CONCRETE
WINNIE—	:	:	:	:	:	:	CORA—
THINKS 95% OF							WOULD BE READY
COUNTRY SHOULD							TO PAVE EVERY-
REMAIN "FOREVER							THING OVER IF IT
WILD," WITH 5%							WOULD STIMULATE
FOR POPULATED							ECONOMIC DEVEL-
AREAS							OPMENT

27. How many friends do you need?

STUCK-UP STANLEY	:	:	:	:	:	:	FRIENDLY FRANK—
—ONLY ONE							WANTS EVERYONE
FRIEND—HIMSELF.							TO BE HIS FRIEND.
SENDS HIMSELF							SENDS 5 POUNDS OF
VALENTINES							CANDY TO EVERY-
							ONE IN THE
							SCHOOL

28. How patriotic are you?

GRIPING GERTIE—	:	:	:	:	:	:	STARS 'N' STRIPES
MY COUNTRY'S							STELLA—MY COUN-
ALWAYS WRONG							TRY'S NEVER
							WRONG

29. How helpful are you to others?

NASTY NELLIE—	:	:	:	:	:	:	SUGAR-SWEET SUE
WOULDN'T DO A							—ALWAYS OFFERS
FAVOR, EVEN FOR							HELP, EVEN WHEN
HER OWN BENEFIT							NOT WANTED

30. How do you feel about seat belts?

WASHY WILLIE—	:	:	:	:	:	:	SCISSORS SAM—
WEARS THEM ALL							CUTS THEM OFF
THE TIME, EVEN							CARS IN PARKING
TO WASH THE CAR							LOTS

31.   How much do you watch TV?

BLURRY-EYED BILL	:	:	:	:	:	:	NO-KNOB NED—
—NEVER TURNS							NEVER TURNS IT ON
IT OFF							

32.   How selective are you about TV?

ANYTHING THAT	:	:	:	:	:	:	EDUCATIONAL
HAPPENS TO BE ON							PROGRAMS ONLY
							OR ENTERTAIN-
							MENT ONLY

33.   What are your newspaper habits?

NEVER LOOK AT	:	:	:	:	:	:	READ EVERY WORD,
ONE, NOT EVEN							FROM COMICS TO
COMICS OR							EDITORIALS
SPORTS PAGES							

34.   How sanitary are you?

DIRTY DENNY—	:	:	:	:	:	:	GERMPROOF GERRY
CHEWS USED							—WASHES HANDS
GUM FROM							BEFORE EACH BITE
UNDERNEATH DESKS							
IN SCHOOL							

35.   How legible is your handwriting?

SCRIBBLY SAM—	:	:	:	:	:	:	CLEAR-AS-PRINT
CAN'T READ							CLARENCE—SPENDS
HIS OWN							HOURS WRITING
WRITING							EVERY HOMEWORK
							ASSIGNMENT

36.   What kind of Halloween celebrant are you?

MISCHIEVOUS MARY	:	:	:	:	:	:	GOODY GERTIE—
—ALL TRICKS,							WOULDN'T TRICK
EVEN AFTER							ANYONE FOR ANY-
TREATS							THING. HAS NEVER
							PLAYED A JOKE ON
							ANYONE IN HER
							WHOLE LIFE.

37.   What kind of Christmas celebrant are you?

GIMME GERTIE—   :   :   :   :   :   : GIVEY GLADYS—
CARES ONLY   GENEROUS TO A
ABOUT WHAT   FAULT. REFUSED
SHE'LL GET   TO OPEN ANY GIFTS
                                            GIVEN TO HER.

38.   What percentage of your waking hours do you like
       to spend alone

                    0 :   :   :   :   :   : 100

STRATEGY NUMBER 9

Spread of Opinion[5]

PURPOSE

Very often with controversial subjects, people tend to see things only in either/or, black or white terms. Along with the values-continuum strategy, this strategy can be used to help students see the wide range of possible positions on any given issue. It asks students to take an even deeper look at various positions than does the values continuum.

PROCEDURE

The teacher breaks the class into groups of five or six. Each group chooses or is assigned a controversial issue. Some sample controversial issues are:

> ABORTION
> POPULATION CONTROL
> WHAT TO DO ABOUT WELFARE
> PREMARITAL SEX
> LEGALIZATION OF MARIJUANA
> DISTRIBUTION OF WEALTH

---

[5]The authors learned this strategy from Louis E. Raths.

COLLEGE ENTRANCE REQUIREMENTS

GRADING SYSTEMS

ENERGY

CORPORATE MARRIAGE

The group then identifies five or six possible positions on their issue. For example, on any of the above issues the students might identify an ultra-conservative stand, a conservative stand, a moderate stand, a liberal stand, a radical stand and a revolutionary stand. Then each student takes one of these positions—not necessarily his own position—and writes a paragraph defending this position. If group members can think of additional positions they may write more than one statement each to cover all these other positions.

When this procedure has been completed, the members of the group reveal their own position and discuss the issue. If all the groups in the class were working on the same issue, each group's continuum is displayed for all to see and a class discussion may follow.

Sometimes after the group has written in defense of arbitrarily selected positions, each group member takes the stand that comes closest to his own real opinion and rewrites or adds to the paragraph so that it most clearly expresses his own viewpoint. The paragraph may be dittoed and handed out to everyone in the class.

Another variation is to have spreads of opinion of all the groups on all the issues posted on the walls; the class can walk around the room viewing each group's work.

Then each member of the class may be given a chance to state aloud his own position on any of the issues.

TO THE TEACHER

This is an excellent strategy to use when you sense the class is thinking very narrowly and unimaginatively about an issue that has come up.

STRATEGY NUMBER 10

Values Whips[6]

PURPOSE

The values whip is much like voting (Strategy Number 3) and ranking (Strategy Number 4) in that it provides a simple and rapid means for students and teacher to see how others react to various issues or questions. Typically, values-whip questions deal with one of the seven valuing processes: seeking *alternatives*, evaluating the *consequences* of alternatives, *choosing freely*, *prizing* choices or actions, *affirming* choices or actions, *acting* upon choices, and developing a *pattern* of behavior.

PROCEDURE

The teacher or a student poses a question to the class and provides a few moments for the members to think about their answers. Then the teacher whips around the room calling upon students to give their answers. The answers should be brief and to the point, although sometimes a

---

[6]The authors learned this strategy from Merrill Harmin, director of the NEXTEP Program, Southern Illinois University, Edwardsville, Illinois.

student may want to give a little background to better explain his answer. Students may choose to pass.

SAMPLE QUESTIONS

1. What is something you are proud of?

2. What is some issue about which you have taken a public stand recently?

3. What was a recent decision you made that involved consideration of three or more alternatives?

4. What is something you really believe in strongly?

ADDITIONAL SUGGESTIONS

1. What is one thing you would change in our world? In your town? Your school? Your neighborhood?

2. What is one thing you hope your own children will not have to go through?

3. What is one thing about which you have changed your mind recently?

4. Who is one person you know who seems to have it "more together" than you? What can you borrow from his life?

5. How did you handle a recent disagreement?

6. What would you have Ralph Nader work on next?

7. What could you give, personally, to the Presidential candidate of your choice?

8.   What is one issue on which you have not yet formed a definite opinion?

9.   Who is the fairest adult you know? What is his or her secret?

10. In your opinion, what should black people (or white people) be doing about integration?

11. What do you want to do about racism?

12. What is something in the news that really disturbed you lately?

13. Which local issue disturbs you?

14. Where do you want to be twenty years from now?

15. How much time do you spend worrying about nuclear warfare?

16. Would you be willing to limit car usage in order to reduce noise and pollution?

17. What one quality do you want in a friend?

18. What is something you really want to learn how to do before you die?

19. What are two places you must see this year?

20. What would you do if you objected to a new school policy?

Other questions for values whips may be found among the public interview questions (Strategy Number 12).

STRATEGY NUMBER 11

Proud Whip

PURPOSE

The Proud Whip is a variation of the Values Whip (Strategy Number 10). Past experience has proven it to be one of the most used and most valuable strategies employed by teachers who have been trained in values clarification. We therefore want to call it to the readers' attention by focusing upon it as an independent strategy. It helps students become more aware of the degree to which they are proud of their beliefs and actions and this will encourage them to do more things in which they can take pride. Students also hear new alternatives from their classmates' lives.

PROCEDURE

The teacher asks students to consider what they have to be proud of in relation to some specific area or issue. The teacher whips around the room calling upon students in order. Students respond with the words, "I'm proud of . . . ." or "I'm proud that. . . ." Any student may pass if he chooses.

SAMPLE QUESTIONS

1. What is something you are proud of that you can do on your own?

2. What is something you are proud of in relation to money?

3. What are you proud of that has to do with school?

4. What are you proud of about your gift giving?

5. What is something you have written that you are proud of?

6. What are you proud of in relation to your family?

7. What is something you have done about the ecology issue that you're proud of?

TO THE TEACHER

You should emphasize that the type of pride that is called for here is not the boastful or bragging kind of pride, but the pride that means, "I feel really good about" or "I cherish" this aspect of life.

The teacher must be very supportive of those who pass. No one should be expected to be proud of everything. Sometimes the teacher deliberately selects an issue that he has to pass on, just to illustrate this point.

Students should be encouraged to volunteer to bring in topics for Proud Whips.

ADDITIONAL EXAMPLES   (I am proud of...
I am proud that...)

1. Any new skill you have learned within the last month or year....

2. Something you did that did not take physical courage, but which you are proud of....

3. A decision that you made which required considerable thought....

4. The completion of a task that was very laborious, but which you stuck out....

5. Some family tradition you are particularly proud of

6. Something you refrained from doing about which you're proud....

7. Anything you've done for an older person....

8. A time when you said something when it would have been easier to remain silent....

9. A time when you didn't say something when it would have been easier to say something....

10. An athletic feat you did recently which you are proud of....

11. Anything you've made with your own hands....

12. A time recently when you made a shrewd purchase or got a good bargain....

13. A habit you worked to overcome, and succeeded . . . .

14. Anything you've done about increasing your repertoire of responses to a situation . . . .

15. A time you were especially loving to someone and about which you feel proud . . . .

16. Anything you did to resist conformity . . . .

17. Anything you did to conform when everyone around you was resisting conformity . . . .

18. A dangerous thing you tried and succeeded at . . . .

19. A conversation, recently, in which you held nothing back, but told exactly where you were at . . . .

20. A new learning about which you feel proud . . . .

21. A way in which you helped your family . . . .

22. Anything you did to contribute to racial understanding . . . .

23. Something you did to *live* by your religion . . . .

24. Anything you've done to add to the store of beauty in this world . . . .

25. Something you've done to add to the quantity of love in this world . . . .

26. A way in which you helped make democracy mean more than a word . . . .

27. Anything you've *done* to support your stand on developing a world community, whatever your stand is. . . .

28. Something you did for someone else which was extremely tender. . . .

29. A funny thing you did about which you are proud . . . .

30. A time when you were an important example for a younger child. . . .

Below are some examples of Proud Whip questions for younger children:

1. I am proud that on my own I can. . . .

2. I am proud that I spent my allowance on. . . .

3. I am proud that when I am scared I. . . .

4. When I watch TV I am proud that. . . .

5. I am proud that I made my friend happy by. . . .

6. I was proud that even when the other kids did. . . . I. . . .

7. I am proud that this summer I. . . .

8. Something my family has done all together this year which made me proud. . . .

9. I am proud that I use my toys. . . .

10.   I am proud of what I did about. . . .

11.   I am proud when the other kids say that. . . .

12.   I'm proud that I made. . . .

13.   I'm proud that I helped keep my city clean by. . . .

14.   I am proud that I keep healthy by. . . .

15.   I'm proud that I helped make my school a happier place. . . .

16.   I'm proud that my father (mother). . . .

STRATEGY NUMBER 12

Public Interview

PURPOSE

This strategy gives the student center stage in the classroom and the opportunity to publicly affirm and explain his stand on various values issues. Later on, inevitably, the student goes over his answers in his mind and thoughtfully considers what he has said publicly. It is one of the most dramatic values strategies and one of the students' favorites.

PROCEDURE

The teacher asks for volunteers who would like to be interviewed publicly about some of their beliefs, feelings and actions. The volunteers sit at the teacher's desk or in a chair in front of the room, and the teacher moves to the back of the room and asks the questions from there.

The first few times, the teacher reviews the ground rules. The teacher may ask the student any question about any aspect of his life and values. If the student answers the question, he must answer honestly. However, the student has the option of passing if he does not wish to answer one or more of the questions which the teacher poses. The student can end the interview at any time by simply saying, "Thank you for the interview." In addition, he may, at the completion of the interview ask the teacher any of the same questions that were put to him.

SAMPLE INTERVIEW QUESTIONS
(for general use)

1. Do you get an allowance? What kind? Do you have to do anything for it?

2. Do you go to Sunday school or religion class? Do you enjoy it?

3. What's fun to do with your family?

4. If you could be any age, what age would you like to be?

5. Did you go on a vacation this year? If you could go anywhere in the world you wanted to next year, where would you go?

6. Will you be a cigarette smoker? Why?

7. Do you wish you had a larger family or a smaller family, or is your family just the right size?

8. As you look at the world around you, what is something you sometimes wonder about?

TO THE TEACHER

The Public Interview strategy is especially useful at the beginning of the year for helping students get acquainted with each other on a more personal basis. Each interview should usually be kept rather brief, five to ten minutes at the most, unless everyone is really involved and wants to hear more. With younger children the interview period should be even shorter.

The teacher can use the interview questions suggested here or make up his own. He may find it helpful to write the questions on a 3×5 card. Above all, the teacher must listen to what the student answers and show he is interested. The best questions, in the long run, are not prearranged ones, but the ones that occur to the teacher spontaneously as he looks at the interviewee and thinks about what he is saying.

When students are being asked questions in front of the class, they often can't remember the questions you asked them when it is their turn to ask you questions. It sometimes helps to allow the other students to remind the interviewee of the questions you asked. ("Ask him the one about. . . .")

Too many questions back to the teacher may take the focus off the student interviewee. Some teachers set a limit of three on the number of questions the student can ask back. Some teachers do not have each student ask questions back. Instead, they sometimes volunteer to be interviewed by one of the students.

Occasionally, the teacher may invite other members of the class to answer any of the questions the interviewee was asked.

As the teacher becomes more adept at conducting the interview, he might suggest that students select the topic they would like to be interviewed about. If the teacher has posted a list of areas of confusion and conflict (see list given at beginning of this book), this will be a rich source of questions for both the student and the teacher.

Sometimes, instead of conducting the interview himself, the teacher may select a student to conduct the interview. Care should be taken, however, to select students who know the ground rules well and are sensitive to and considerate of their classmates' feelings.

ADDITIONAL SUGGESTIONS

Questions for Intermediate and Secondary Students and Adults

1. Do you like to take long walks? Which place do you like to walk to the most?
2. About how much money do you plan to spend on Christmas gifts this year? Is that more or less than last year?
3. Do you watch TV much? How much?
4. What is your opinion on public welfare? (or any other political issue the teacher may think is appropriate)

5. How many hours of sleep do you get on the average each night? What effect do you think this has on your life style?

6. Do you have a personal motto you live by?

7. What is your stand on the birth control pill?

8. How much do you like to give to charities, causes, etc.?

9. Whom will you support in the coming election?

10. What is your stand on smoking?

11. How do you feel about grades in school?

12. What do you plan on doing this (Thanksgiving, Easter, Christmas, summer)vacation ?

13. What parts of nature do you love the most?

14. Have you ever made a choice that surprised everyone?

15. Do you have a role model? What is it about him/her you admire?

16. Should your school give seniors full birth control information?

17. What is one thing you would like to learn before you die?

18. How do you deal with unpleasant aspects of your work, or of school?

19. What brand of toothpaste do you use? How did you come to use that brand?

20. Who was your best friend before the best friend you now have?

21. Did you ever write a letter to the editor? What was the topic?

22. How important are engagement rings to you?

23. What are you saving money for?

24. Do you buy many records? What kind? Where do you get the money?

25. Are you more or less religious now than you were three years ago?

26. Have you ideas about what you would like to do when you are an adult?

27. What possibilities for your future have you talked over with your parents?

28. How do you feel when you visit a hospital?

29. If you could learn a new skill, what would it be?

30. What is one thing that you hope to continue doing throughout your life?

31. Is there any particular organization or club you want to belong to? Why?

32. How do you spend your time after school?

33. Of all the things you do in your free time, which do you like most?

34. Which of your free-time activities do you like least?

35. What does your family usually do for Thanksgiving? Christmas?

36. What have you done the last two Thanksgiving vacations?

37. What have you done the last two Christmas vacations?

38. What magazines do you read regularly?

39. Do you subscribe to any magazines yourself?

40. What are your favorite TV shows?

41. Have you seen any movies in the last few months which you liked?

42. Tell me in a sentence or two about a movie you

saw and why you liked it.

43. What are your favorite sports?
44. What books have you read that you liked?
45. Do you work after school or on Saturdays? Where? What are you using the money for?
46. What do you like best about school?
47. What do you like least about school?
48. If you could change some part of your educational program, what would it be?
49. If you were a teacher, how would you teach your classes?
50. Have you a hobby which takes up a lot of your time? What is it?
51. How did you get interested in your hobby?
52. Are your friends interested in the same hobby as you?
53. Are some of your friends not interested in your hobby?
54. Is there an adult outside of school whom you dislike intensely? Why?
55. Are there some adults outside of school whom you admire intensely? Why?
56. Have you ever invented anything? What?
57. What is there about you which makes your friends like you?
58. Is there something you want badly but can't afford right now? What?
59. Of all the people you know who have helped you, who has helped the most? How did he/she go about it?

60. What are some things you really believe in?

61. Where did you spend the best summer of your life?

62. If you could change your school, what two things would you change?

63. What is the worst work you have done for money?

64. What do you see yourself doing five years from now? Ten years? Twenty?

65. Are there injustices in your community you feel need attention?

66. Do you send any money to charities? Which ones? Which ones do you object to supporting?

67. What is the most important book or movie or play you've read or seen in the past year?

68. What one thing would you change about yourself if you could?

69. What is a difficult choice you face right now in your life?

70. Do you believe in burial, cremation, or what?

71. What is one action you've taken to make this world more beautiful?

72. Do you wear seat belts?

73. What are some of your notions of the good life?

74. Do you smoke?

75. Do you have full polio protection?

76. Are there things you would not tell even best friends? What kinds of things?

77. What is the most serious environmental concern you have today?

78. How do you feel about going steady?

79. Do you ever do things to make your parents feel good without their having asked you? What? When?

80. Did you ever steal something? When? How come?

81. Do you ever get teased? Do you ever tease others?

82. Describe the best teacher you ever had.

83. How have you enjoyed school over the years?

84. What makes you dislike a person on sight?

85. Can you think of something that you would like to say to the group that you think might be good for them to hear?

86. Do you feel satisfied with your life?

87. What improvements would you like to make in your life?

88. What would you consider your main interests in life?

89. Describe something you have done recently to a person you dislike.

90. What do you do when you want to get out of something?

91. If you had an extra $500 given to you with no strings attached, what would you do with it?

92. Would you like to marry? Soon?

93. In your estimation, what are the values of funerals?

94. How many children would you like to have?

95. How do you feel about interracial marriage?

96. How do you feel about homosexuality?

97. Which celebrity would you like to have for a friend?

98. What is one thing you could stop doing to help lessen the energy crisis?

99. What is your favorite color?

100. Are you satisfied with your height?

101. As a child, did you ever run away from home? Did you ever want to?

102. Do you think you were an obedient child?

103. What was the most frightening thing that ever happened to you?

104. Do you believe in life after death?

105. How often do you get into trouble?

106. How do you handle it when you get into trouble?

107. How do you think teachers should dress in school?

108. What do you consider the worst thing you ever did?

109. Do you have a favorite food?

110. How often do you eat out?

111. Do you ever cook? What do you make?

112. What is one idea, skill, or article you have passed on this past year?

113. Who are the other people in your family?

114. Describe one of the people in your family in two sentences.

115. What present would you like to get?

116. Do you do things spontaneously or do you think things through before doing anything?

117. Do you ever do things just because others expect you to do them that way?

118. Should people always do what they like to do?

119. How do you know when something is right or wrong?

120. Do you think a person should tell another person about somthing personal and embarrassing—such as bad breath or soiled clothes?

121. If someone embarrassed you, what would you do?

122. Do you enjoy your pace of life at present? Would you like to speed it up or slow it down?

123. What do you think of the new morality?

124. Do you feel the problems of pollution are being ex-aggerated?

125. If you could change one thing during your lifetime, what would it be?

126. Do you get enough money for your allowance?

127. Are you proud of being a girl? (A boy?)

128. Would you tell your best friend he has bad breath?

129. Have you experienced death close to you?

130. Would you marry someone of another race?

131. Do you have faith in our political system?

132. Are you proud of your work habits?

133. Do you practice your religion?

134. Can you tell your parents your personal problems?

135. How would you feel about calling your teacher by his/her first name?

136. What are three things you are good at?

137. What, if any, career goals do you have?

138. Have you ever written a letter to a company com-plaining about a product?

139. What is one event that took place in your life that made a big difference?

140. How much TV do you watch?

141. Have you ever tried to return a product to a store because it was defective?

142. Do you feel your teachers are fair?

143. What is something interesting people might never know about you?

144. What is your most prized possession?

145. What do you enjoy most in life?

146. Are you planning to go to college?

147. Are you good at getting high grades?

148. What would you do if you got too much change given to you at the checkout counter?

149. Do you think social studies books should have more about black history?

150. Have you ever signed a peition? For what?

151. Have you ever been on a motorcycle? Would you wear a helmet even if it were not the law?

152. Are you curious about trying pot?

153. Have you ever carried a picket sign?

154. What makes your best friend your best friend?

155. Do you know how to keep a checking account?

156. What is the one thing you want to learn how to do better?

157. Do you ever treat other kids to food?

158. Did you ever cheat at Monopoly?

159. Do you like to get letters? To write letters?

160. Which was your best year in school?

161. Do you think you will ever dye your hair? Are you prejudiced against women or men who do?

162. If you were driving in the country at night and you

came to a red light which didn't change for some time, what would you do?

163. In what ways are you a conformist?

164. Have you ever read a book which had a deep effect in your life?

165. Did you spend any time last summer flat on your back looking for falling stars?

166. Do you think you're very materialistic?

167. What would you suggest to make this a better school?

168. Would you work actively to improve your school?

Questions for Younger Children

Interviews with younger children should not run too long. Between 10 and 20 questions is probably enough. The following are typical interview sequences for younger children:

1. What present would you give your mother for her birthday? Your father?

2. What did you like about your summer vacation?

3. What was the scariest TV show you ever watched? Do you still watch it? Who was the advertiser? What was advertised? Will you buy the product?

4. Do you and your parents enjoy watching the same TV programs?

5. How many pairs of shoes do you have? Who bought them?
6. Do you think you will grow a beard when you grow up? Let your hair grow long? Bleach your hair?
7. Do you wish your teacher were a different kind of person? How?
8. What did you have for breakfast? What is your favorite breakfast? How often do you have this? Have you ever had a day when you could ask for anything you wanted to eat?
9. Do you know any kids who shoplift?
10. What's the fastest you have ever been driven in a car?

1. Do you get an allowance?
2. Do you go to Sunday school or religion class?
3. Do you litter? Why? Why not?
4. Why do you think your friends like you?
5. Are you a member of a Brownie Troop? (Cub Pack?)
6. Do you come promptly when you are called?
7. Are you happy that you are a boy? (A girl?)
8. Do you feel that you do your best work all the time?
9. Would you like to be older or younger than you are now?
10. Did you go on a vacation this year?

1. Do you wish you had an older sister? Brother?
2. Is your best friend a boy or a girl?
3. Would you like to be a patrol monitor?

4. What makes you most angry?
5. Do you ever do anything to earn money?
6. What would you do if you couldn't watch TV?
7. Do you like making new friends?
8. Do you think department stores should be open on Sunday?
9. Did you ever write a love letter to a boy (or a girl)?
10. Are you expected to do certain chores around the house?

1. What is the happiest thing you can remember?
2. What is the saddest thing you can remember?
3. What wish would you make?
4. Who is your closest friend?
5. What do you like best about your closest friend?
6. What do you dislike about your closest friend?
7. Would you tell your closest friend what you don't like about him? (Her?)
8. If you could visit any place in the world, where would you go?
9. Tell me three things you like to do best.
10. Tell me three things you like to do least. Rank them.
11. If you could have $100 cash, what would you do with it?

1. Have you ever been very sick?
2. Are you enjoying school?
3. What do you like to do after school?
4. Do you like being inside or outside more?

5. Do you like to walk?
6. Do you like babies? Why?
7. Is there something that you once did that you are especially proud of?
8. Do you have a special place of your own?
9. Can you tell us one nice thing about yourself?
10. Can you tell us one bad habit that you have?
11. Do you like daytime or nighttime better?
12. What is your favorite dessert?
13. Do you like to climb trees? Ice skate? Go to the movies?
14. Would you like to fly a plane?
15. Would you like to ask *me* any questions?

Here are 50 questions used during many interviews by one third-grade teacher.

1. What is your full name? Do you like it? Would you change it if you could?
2. Do you have any brothers or sisters? How do you get along?
3. Do you ever daydream? What about?
4. What do you do around the house in the way of chores?
5. Do you get an allowance? Is it fair? What do you do with it?
6. Are you rich? Do you want to get rich when you grow up?

7. How do people get rich? Why are some people poor?

8. Do you like to be teased? How does it make you feel?

9. How do you show your parents that you love them?

10. Would you like to live in the country or in the city?

11. Do you like school? Do you think you'll go to college?

12. What kind of work do you want to do when you grow up?

13. Would you like to get married? What kind of person would you choose?

14. Would you make a good husband/wife?

15. How many children do you think you'll want?

16. Do you have any friends of different religions or races?

17. Are you allowed to make a lot of your own decisions at home? About what?

18. Who decides how you should wear your hair? What clothes you should wear?

19. What's your favorite ice cream flavor?

20. Did you ever ask your parents where babies come from?

21. Would you like to be an author some day?

22. Do you have any hobbies?

23. How much time do you spend watching TV? What are your favorite TV shows?

24. How often do you go to the movies?

25. What book have you read that you liked very much?
26. Do you think you'd make a good teacher?
27. If you were a teacher, would you be strict?
28. Is there someone you dislike a lot? Why?
29. What is there about you that makes your friends like you?
30. Do you have one close friend or many friends?
31. Would you want a black person (white person) for your neighbor?
32. Would you invite a black person (white person) to your house for dinner?
33. Would you join the army?
34. Do you think you'll smoke some day?
35. Why do you think some people take dope?
36. What would you do if you found some money in the street?
37. Do you have a pet?
38. Do you want a big wedding?
39. Do you like to eat sweets?
40. Do you buy or bring your lunch?
41. Have you ever stolen anything?
42. Is there something special you want for your birthday?
43. Do you ever have trouble falling asleep?
44. Did you ever cheat on tests?
45. If you could go anywhere in the world, where would you like to go?
46. Are you ever alone in the house? How often? How do you feel?

47. What time do you go to bed? Who decides?
48. Have you ever made anything? What?
49. What do you think happens to people after they die?
50. Do you have your own room at home? If not, who shares it with you?

STRATEGY NUMBER 13

The Interview Whip and Interview Chain[7]

PURPOSE

These two strategies are major variations on the Public Interview (Strategy Number 12). Their purpose is to give students additional opportunities for publicly stating and explaining their views.

PROCEDURE

In the Interview Whip, the teacher "whips" around the classroom, in order or randomly, asking interview questions of each student. He may ask several students the same question, or he may choose to ask a different question each time.

In the Interview Chain, the teacher starts out the chain by addressing an interview question to a student. After answering, that student must then ask another student an interview question, and the chain continues in this manner.

---

[7]The authors learned these variations on the Public Interviews from Merrill Harmin.

A student may always pass. In the Interview Chain, a student who passes may still ask a question if he wishes. There is never a penalty for passing.

TO THE TEACHER

The questions suggested for Public Interview are just as appropriate for these two strategies. But, as with the Public Interview, many of the best questions come spontaneously, as the interviewer follows his curiosity about the interviewee, or as he gets an idea from an answer given to a previous question.

STRATEGY NUMBER 14

Group Interview

PURPOSE

This strategy, done in small groups, provides students with an opportunity to share on a more intimate basis than in the Public Interview (Strategy Number 12) some of their personal interests, beliefs, activities and values. It also affords the students the experience of interviewing each other.

PROCEDURE

The teacher has the students break into groups of five to ten. One member of the group volunteers to be interviewed by the group. Before the interview starts, group members take a minute or two to write down any questions they would like to ask the focus person. The volunteer may also write down questions he would like to be asked; he passes these to a friend. The questions should deal with his interests, hobbies, family, friends, beliefs, hopes, goals in life, activities.

The students ask the focus person questions. The focus controls the interview by calling upon group members as he chooses. He had the option of not answering any question he feels is too personal or inappropriate by saying, "I pass." He may also question a group member about his purpose in asking a question before he chooses to answer it. Unless there is a time limit set, the interview is over when there are no more questions or when the focus ends it by saying, "Thank you for your questions."

The interview is to be conducted by the following ground rules which are given to the students:

1. Personal information, beliefs and values are to be shared and discussed on a voluntary basis. Please remember that there are things which all of us do not wish to discuss with others at a particular moment. This feeling should be recognized and respected by all members of the group.

2. The group interview is not the place for argument or debate. Please respect each other's right to live differently, feel differently, think differently and value differently. You may disagree with someone in the group; but try to understand his position rather than telling him he is wrong or trying to make him change. People are more apt to change their life styles, beliefs and values when and if they have different experiences, rather than when they are badgered into feeling their ideas are wrong.

TO THE TEACHER

It is best to do several Public Interviews (Strategy Number 12) or Interview Whips (Strategy Number 13) before doing the Group Interview. This enables you to demonstrate the variety of questions that can be asked to set a tone of questioning-out-of-interest rather than questioning-to-attack. To demonstrate the Group Interview procedure you might start with the whole class as one big group and then break up into smaller groups.

STRATEGY NUMBER 15

I Learned Statements[8]

PURPOSE

This strategy serves several purposes. It provides the group and the teacher with feedback about the last activity they participated in. It helps clarify and reinforce what the students have learned. It crystallizes new learnings which many students might not have realized were taking place. It sets a very powerful searching tone in the group. Finally, it provides a good summary or windup for almost any activity.

PROCEDURE

The teacher prepares a chart with the following (or similar) sentence stems. The chart may be posted permanently in the room, or it may be posted just when it is to be used.

I learned that I...   I realized that I...

---

[8]Our thanks to Jerry Weinstein of the Center for Humanistic Education, University of Massachusetts, for this exercise.

I re-learned that I. . .   I was surprised that I. . .
I noticed that I. . .   I was pleased that I. . .
I discovered that I. . .   I was displeased that I. . .

Right after a values activity or discussion, the teacher asks the students to think for a minute about what they have just learned or re-learned about themselves or their values. Then they are to use any one of the sentence stems to share with the group one or more of their feelings. Students are not called on, but volunteer to speak whenever they feel comfortable about it.

TO THE TEACHER

Sometimes it is helpful the first time around to have students write down a few I Learned Statements before sharing them aloud. It is also helpful if the teacher provides students with one or two examples of I Learned Statements. For example, "I realized that I was not clear about my own religious beliefs." "I was surprised that I felt disappointed when someone gave an opinion about Vietnam that was different from mine."

The teacher should not allow discussion to interrupt the free flow of I Learned Statements; it tends to destroy the mood and intensity of the activity. Statements should be kept short and to the point. Students should make their statements but not attempt to explain or defend them.

Try to help students focus on personal learnings rather than on general, intellectualized learnings. There is a tendency to say, "I learned that people...." rather than "I learned that *I*...."

Reassure the students that there are no right answers. And students should always have the freedom to pass or sit the activity out without saying anything.

If the teacher thinks it advisable, he may break up the class into small groups of from three to five members and have these students share and discuss their I Learned Statements with one another.

Sometimes students can simply compile a list of I Learned Statements in writing which they date and put into their Values Data Bank (Strategy Number 17). It is not always necessary to share these ideas with others.

STRATEGY NUMBER 16

I Wonder Statements[9]

PURPOSE

This rather simple but powerful strategy is designed to help students raise and verbalize questions that may have arisen in their minds. Most of the time, in school, students are called upon to make statements and answer questions. It is extremely important to give them ample opportunity to ask questions if we want to stimulate probing, critical attitudes.

PROCEDURE

Upon completion of a values activity or discussion, the teacher asks students to complete in writing sentences beginning with "I wonder," such as:

I wonder if. . .   I wonder why. . .

I wonder how come. . .   I wonder whether. . .

I wonder about. . .   I wonder when. . .

---

[9]Thanks to Joe Levin for Research for Better Schools in Philadelphia, for the kernel idea in this strategy.

Then the teacher goes round and round the room calling on students to share their I Wonder Statements with the class. Any student may pass, of course. The teacher should participate, too, and might even start it off with an example or two of his own. There is no discussion of the questions raised since the goal is to stimulate inquiry.

TO THE TEACHER

If the interest following a values activity is really intense, you might want to start on the I Wonder Statements orally without allowing a writing period to perhaps detract from the mood.

Occasionally you will find that the first time around yields up only superficial questions, but they usually become more powerful with each successive circle.

STRATEGY NUMBER 17

The Values Journal or The Values Data Bank

PURPOSE

Value-clarification methods encourage students to examine their own lives in the same way that the scientific method helps the scientist explore her area of study. The scientist collects as much information or data as she can about her subject. She tries to understand the data by looking for explanations and patterns. Eventually, she hopes to gain control over her subject of study—whether it is atomic energy or cancer or a new synthetic substance.

In much the same way, the student who is forging his own values places himself under a microscope and studies his own patterns of choosing, prizing and acting. The goal of his search is to make sense out of all the data he has collected about himself in order to achieve direction and control over his own life and be less at the mercy of inner compulsions and external pressures.

The Values Journal, also called the Values-Search Data Bank, provides the student with a simple storage and retrieval system for the information he collects in his search for values.

PROCEDURE

The teacher intrduces the Values Journal by talking about the importance of collecting information about ourselves —about how we choose, what we choose, how we feel about what we choose, and how we act upon our choices. He asks each student to keep a journal or a special section in his notebook for "Values." All the notes from values activities—Privacy Circles, Values Grids, I Learned Statements, etc.—go into this journal or data bank. Students can also use their values journals to jot down values-related thoughts and feelings whenever they occur, in school or out. In other words, like the scientist, the student stores the information he collects about himself in his search for values. The teacher stresses that this is to be the student's own private property and no one will be allowed to look at it, not even the teacher, without the student's permission.

Any student may show his journal to the teacher if he wants to. The teacher may write in his responses, if the student requests it. The student may choose never to show the journal to anyone. He may use it just to help himself clarify his own thinking and for his own reference.

The teacher may, if he thinks it appropriate, set aside part of a file cabinet in the classroom where students could keep their data bank folders. They could go to the file cabinet at appropriate times to file information or the teacher might pass out the folders and then collect them after a values activity.

From time to time, the teacher can ask the students questions about their journals. For example: "Are your values concerns at all different from what they were a month ago? Are you clearer now on any values issues than you were before? Are some issues more confusing?"

Or the teacher may ask the student to read or talk about one item in his journal. Of course, any student may pass. Or some of the students may want to write compositions about an item in their journals.

STRATEGY NUMBER 18

Values Focus Game[10]

PURPOSE

The search for values is facilitated when there is a supportive and accepting environment. To encourage this kind of climate in the classroom, both the teacher and the students must learn to respect each other's right to hold different views and to act in accordance with their different convictions. The Values-Focus Game is designed to help students be open to, accept and understand even if they do not agree with, different points of view. The objective of this activity is to help students understand more effectively another person's point of view, rather than to attempt to change the person's mind through attack or debate.

PROCEDURE

To introduce the game, the teacher has the students complete in writing several stem sentences. Two that work very well in this context are:

---

[10]An adaptation of the Positive-Focus Game developed by Saville Sax, NEXTEP Program, Southern Illinois University, Edwardsville, Illinois.

"I feel best when I am in a group of people that
. . . ."

"I feel worst when I am in a group of people that
. . . ."

After each student has completed his unfinished sentences,
the teacher asks the class to arrange themselves into
groups of three. Each student in the group is to have the
focus—the full attention of the other two group members—for a period of five minutes. During this period the
focus person is to talk about his responses. The group's interaction is to be governed by the following rules:

1. *The Rule of Focusing.* Each group member is to be
   the focus person for a period of five minutes. Do not let
   the attention of the group shift from the focus person
   until his time is up or until he asks to stop. Maintain
   eye contact with the focus person at a comfortable level. Questions may be asked of the focus person if they
   do not shift the focus to another group member.

2. *The Rule of Acceptance.* Be warm, supportive and
   accepting of the focus person. Nods, smiles and expressions of understanding when sincerely given help communicate acceptance. If you do not agree with the
   focus person, do not express disagreement or negative
   feelings during the discussion part of the game. There
   will be time for this later on.

3. *The Rule of Drawing Out.* Attempt to understand the
   focus person's position, feelings and beliefs. Ask questions which will help to clarify the reasons for the focus

person's feelings. Make sure that your questions do not shift the focus to yourself, or reveal negative feelings which you may have about the focus person or about what he is saying.

Each student is provided with a copy of the rules and the teacher explains them fully.

TO THE TEACHER

The Values-Focus Game can be used with almost any values activity that requires small group discussion. It really teaches listening. The rule of focusing can be dropped, if need be, to facilitate a more free-floating discussion.

Upon completion of the game, especially the first few times, the teacher may suggest that students rate themselves and each other, on a five-point scale, to assess how well they were able to follow the three rules. These rates should then be shared and discussed in the small group with the intent of helping students become more proficient at really listening to others and understanding their feelings and ideas.

After the students have rated themselves and each other on how well they listened, time can be taken for students to react to each other's positions. They voice their agreement or disagreement, and discuss their various points of view.

STRATEGY NUMBER 19

—Ing Name Tags

PURPOSE

This strategy asks participants to look more closely at what they value and who they are. Second, it asks them to publicly affirm these aspects of themselves. And third, it is an easy way to help a new group—no matter how large—relax a bit and begin to get acquainted.

PROCEDURE

The teacher gives every student a large (e.g. 5 × 7) index card or piece of paper and a safety or straight pin. He asks every student to write his first name with crayon or marker in large letters on the card so it will be visible across the room. Then they are to write five or six words ending in "ing" which tell something about who they are, e.g., piano-playing, reading, fun-loving, fighting, base-balling, etc. They should write these words anywhere on their cards on the same side as their names.

Then the teacher asks them to turn their cards over and write their names again, in big letters. This time they are to write five or six words that report specific facts or statistics about themselves. They might write their addresses, phone numbers, height, number of brothers or sisters, last names, etc.

When they have completed both sides, the teacher asks them to choose the side they will expose to the group. The students then fasten their tags to their clothes.

The teacher asks everyone to get up and mill about the room in random fashion, reading each other's name tags, looking at clothes, eyes, faces; shaking hands, and asking questions if they feel like it. The teacher can ask that this be done with or without words. Of course, he participates too.

VARIATIONS

Instead of —ing words, other stems which can be used are:

- —able (touchable, reasonable, breakable, lovable, improvable)
- —ful (beautiful, trustful, wasteful, angerful, spiteful)
- —ist (optimist, botanist, cyclist, realist, specialist)
- —less (careless, penniless, merciless, hopeless, errorless)

TO THE TEACHER

Encourage students to feel free to make up their own words or modify words. You might ask them to write additional information on their name tags—a hero, a place they'd like to live, two things they think about, etc.

STRATEGY NUMBER 20

Partner Risk or Sharing Trios

PURPOSE

One of the seven valuing processes is self-disclosure—a willingness to openly state and to stand up for our beliefs and actions. Learning to build trust so that we can risk being open is fundamental to this process. Partner Risk or Sharing Trios is a step in this direction.

PROCEDURE

The teacher asks students to pick one or two partners whom they do not know very well. For five minutes, each student is to share with his partner(s) the high point and the low point in his life during the past week—that is, they are each to tell what was most satisfying in the week and what was least satisfying. When five minutes are up, each student finds another partner whom he does not know very well. The new pairs are then given a new topic to discuss for five minutes. (See suggested topics below.) This procedure may be repeated several times.

Following one or more five-minute discussion periods, the teacher asks the students to close their eyes and think about the following questions:

1. Were you really listened to? Did your partner really hear you? Did you listen to him/her?

2. Did you really share your feelings or did you screen them before talking about them?

3. Did you worry that you talked too much? Too little?

4. Were you mostly a "pickee" (one who was chosen by another when partners were switched), or a "picker" (one who did the choosing)? Suggestion: Next time reverse roles. If you were a "pickee," try to be a "picker." Which would you rather be?

5. Would you have added to your discussion if you had had more time?

6. Was your partner like you or quite different from you? Can you understand him? Do you like having a partner who is like you? Different from you?

7. Would you like your partner to have some of your experiences? Would you like to have some of his/hers?

SUGGESTED TOPICS FOR FIVE MINUTE DISCUSSIONS:

1. Share the high point of last Thanksgiving or the low point of last Christmas.

2. Share something about a hero of yours, either living or dead.

3. Share an experience you have had with a "Dear John" letter you have sent or received, or a letter you have written to the editor.

4. Share your opinion on the illegal use of drugs or on premarital sex.

TO THE TEACHER

If a student has nothing to discuss about the assigned topic, he may pass. If he wishes to substitute a topic for the one given, he may do so.

This is an especially good exercise to use with a new group. It builds rapport rapidly.

Additional suggestions for topics for Partner-Risk or Sharing-Trios discussions:

1. What are some things you do which you think are quite unconventional?

2. Tell about a turning point in your life.

3. Describe a time of your greatest despair.

4. Tell about the person who had the most tremendous impact upon your life.

5. Tell something about some political involvement which meant a great deal to you.

6. Tell some things that you would put in your will.

7. Describe a social evening which is the worst kind for you and tell what you do about it.

8. Tell where you stand on the topic of masturbation.

9. Share the most intense religious experience of your life.

10. Tell about a situation in which you felt very embarrassed.

11. Expound on your views about engagement rings.

12. Name three ways in which your present love relationship would be better if only the other person would. . . .

13. Tell about some of the beautiful things your family does in the realm of ritual.

14. Tell how you feel and what you actually do about alcohol or pot.

15. Share a superstition you hold.

16. Disclose one area in your life where you have settled for less than you had once wanted.

17. Share some of your experiences with or feelings about death.

18. Tell in as much detail as possible just what you consider the most satisfactory way to handle your burial.

19. Tell, with as much honesty as possible, whether you really prefer to be loved more than you can love back, or to love more than you are loved back.

20. Reveal who in your family brings you the greatest sadness, and why. Then share who brings you the greatest joy.

The following topics are for younger children:

1. Tell about a time when you were really needed by someone.

2. Tell about a time when you felt you were being left out of a group.

3. Tell about the first time you felt you loved someone who was not in your family.

4. Talk about a tender who really frightened you or hurt your feelings.

5. Describe how your life might change if there were no TV.

6. Talk about some of the things that confuse you about this world.

7. Talk about your allowance—how much you get, when and how, and whether you think it's fair.

8. Tell about a time when you were deeply misunderstood.

9. Tell about a movie which touched you deeply.

10. Describe what you are sure you don't want to be like when you grow up.

11. Talk about one or more things you would like to be able to do better socially, or intellectually, or athletically, or as a family member, or as a citizen, or as a friend, etc.

12. Tell how you think this world could be better and what you could do about it.

13. Talk about your favorite sport or game.

14. Describe your best friend, how you met, why you like him/her.

STRATEGY NUMBER 21

Privacy Circles

PURPOSE

Publicly affirming our position or belief, under the appropriate circumstances, is one of the seven sub-processes of valuing. Yet (as is brought out in the Risk Ratio Strategy Number 22), it is often difficult to determine when circumstances are appropriate or inappropriate. The Privacy Circles strategy encourages students to think more about their pattern of self-disclosure and self-containment in relation to their feelings, opinions and actions. It gives students the opportunity to find out whom they are willing to tell what. It often raises the questions: "Am I too open?" and "Am I too closed?"

PROCEDURE

The teacher either gives or asks students to draw a set of privacy circles, as pictured. He then explains what each band represents, starting with the outermost one and moving inwards.

There are some things about our lives we would be glad to let anyone, even strangers, know—our favorite TV

show, the type of hat we like to wear, our address. Other
things we might not want strangers to know, but we
would tell to acquaintances, such as our classmates or our
business associates or a neighbor. Still other things we
would reserve only for our friends. Then there are
thoughts and feelings we have, or things we've done or do
that we would tell only our most intimate friends, perhaps our best boyfriend or girlfriend or a spouse. Finally, there may be some aspects of our lives we would not
want to share with anyone; these are reserved only for
ourselves. (The last small circle is darkened to acknowl-
edge that there are some feelings or facts that we don't
admit even to ourselves.)

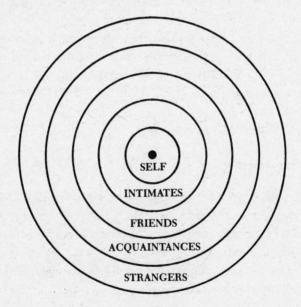

Then the teacher asks the students to write two things (beliefs, feelings or actions) about themselves for each band of the circle. In the friends' band, for example, they write two things they would tell their friends and intimates, not acquaintances or strangers.

Next the teacher asks the students a series of questions like, "Who is your choice for _____ in the coming election?" Instead of answering the question, the students write the key word of the question, "election," in the band which shows to whom they would be willing to reveal their answer. The teacher asks about five or six of these questions, such as:

1. You have had extramarital sexual experience. (Key word: *Extramarital*)
2. Your doubts about religion. (Key word: *Doubts*)
3. What you spend your money on. (Key word: *Money*)
4. The story of your first love. (Key word: *Love*)
5. What you dislike about your best friend. (Key word: *Friend*)

TO THE TEACHER

Blocks or squares may be used instead of circles. They are easier to draw and to write on.

As a follow-up activity, the teacher might ask the students to write a paragraph or short essay on "What I'm Willing to Publicly Affirm" or "Public Affirmation, Privacy and Me." The class might also do I Learned or I Wonder Statements (Strategies Number 15 and 16).

ADDITIONAL SUGGESTIONS

To whom would you tell:

1. You have had extramarital sexual experience. (Key word: *Extramarital*)

2. Your salary. (Key word: *Salary*)

3. You have had premarital sexual relations. (Key word: *Premarital*)

4. Your innermost desires. (Key word: *Desires*)

5. Your personal problems. (Key word: *Problems*)

6. Your health problems. (Key word: *Health*)

7. Your pet likes and dislikes. (Key word: *Likes*)

8. You cheat on your income tax. (Key word: *Cheat*)

9. The amount of income tax you pay. (Key word: *Income Tax*)

10. Whom you vote for. (Key word: *Vote*)

11. You have considered suicide. (Key word: *Suicide*)

12. You smoke marijuana. (Key word: *Marijuana*)

13. You use illegal drugs. (Key word: *Drugs*)

14. You have had an abortion. (Key word: *Abortion*)

15. Your doubts about religion. (Key word: *Religious Doubts*)

16. The major problem(s) in your marriage. (Key word: *Marriage Problems*)

17. You had a check that bounced. (Key word: *Bounced*)

18. You slapped a child. (Key word: *Slapped*)

19. The exact cost of your house. (Key word: *House*)

20. About any racist tendencies you might have. (Key word: *Racist*)

21. What you cried about the last time. (Key word: *Cried*)

22. When you experienced very profound jealousy. (Key word: *Jealousy*)

23. Your method of birth control. (Key word: *Birth Control*)

24. Your discontent with some part of your body. (Key word: *Body*)

25. About cheating or apple-polishing during your high school and college years. (Key word: *Grade-grubbing*)

SOME PRIVACY CIRCLE QUESTIONS FOR YOUNGER CHILDREN:
(Key words are in italics)

1. Whom would you tell that you cried when you were left *alone?*

2. To whom would you mention that you had a *scary dream?*

3. With whom would you share that you had once *taken money* from your dad's dresser, or from your mother's pocketbook?

4. To whom would you say that you are really *good at something*—like playing first base, or jumping rope or some other skill like that?

5. To whom would you say that you are really *bad at something* like ice-skating, baseball, math, etc.?

6. To whom would you admit that there is a *superstition* that you have?

7. Which people would you tell exactly what your *favorite meal* is?

8. Whom would you tell that you once saw something you think you *shouldn't have seen?*

9. Whom would you tell that you once did something *mean* to an animal?

10. In which circle would you write the name of your *best friend?*

STRATEGY NUMBER 22

Risk Ratio
or Force-Field Analysis

PURPOSE

This activity, like Privacy Circles (Strategy Number 21), is intended to help students determine what are the proper circumstances for publicly affirming their ideas, feelings, actions. There are times when it would be suicidal or counterproductive to make public affirmations of our values. Sometimes such affirmations would make it more difficult to work for other values we hold. Yet, sometimes not to affirm our position is nothing other than cowardice or taking the easy way out. How can we tell the difference?

"If I tell my colleagues what I really think about Issue Number 1, I may be ostracized, and then I lose my power to influence positive changes on Issues 2, 3, and 4. Is it worth the risk?"

"I don't want to do what my friends do every Saturday night. Should I tell them and risk losing my membership in this group?"

"I'd like to tell my boyfriend what bothers me about something he does, but I'm scared he'll get mad at me or that it will mean the end of our relationship. Is it worth the risk?"

"I'd like to tell my teacher what I think of his methods, but my grade may suffer. Is it worth the risk?"

This strategy uses the popular Force-Field Analysis to evaluate the risks in making a public affirmation.

PROCEDURE

The teacher gives a few examples of some public affirmation conflicts which he or the students might face. Then he asks them to write on the top of a piece of paper an opinion or feeling they have had that they would like to affirm—to their community, to the class, to a teacher, to their family, to their friends, to their boy- or girlfriend. It should be an opinion or feeling which they would have some difficulty expressing—which involves some risk.

They are then instructed to draw a line down the middle of the paper. On the left-hand side of the paper they are to list all the advantages or benefits to be gained if an affirmation were made. On the right-hand side they are to list all the disadvantages or costs or risks which might result if an affirmation were made. Then, after comparing the list of benefits against the list of costs, either privately or with a partner, they are to write at the bottom of the paper whether they think the risk is worth taking; and, if it is, whether or not they plan on taking any action at this point.

TO THE TEACHER

The teacher might suggest that a helpful technique for comparing the costs against the benefits is to look for listings on either side which have equal weight and would cancel each other out. Or it may be that they will find two costs that cancel out one of the benefits. As listings are canceled a line should be drawn through them. Finally the student will be left with more items on one side of his list than on the other. This should help him in making a decision.

Each advantage and each risk could be given a numerical value on a scale from one to ten. Thus, a ratio of the advantages over the risks could be derived. A ratio greater than one would indicate the risk is worth taking. Conversely, a ratio of less than one would indicate the risk is not worth taking. It should be pointed out, however, that since the point value given each advantage or risk is entirely subjective, there is nothing objectively accurate about this procedure. Its value is in helping students measure their own feelings about the pros and cons of the dilemma.

The use of the Force-Field Analysis, which stems from the work of Kurt Lewin, is not limited to the issue of public affirmation. When students, as individuals or as a group, are considering an action that has both advantages and disadvantages the Force-Field Analysis can be used.

The Removing the Barriers to Action Strategy (Number 27) also fits in well here as a way of helping the student reduce the restraining forces, thus making the action more clearly advantageous.

STRATEGY NUMBER 23

Alternatives Search

PURPOSE

When was the last time you made a choice from among more than three alternatives? This is a crucial question in the search for values; for much of the time we make our decisions and live our lives without looking at all the possible alternatives.

This activity is designed to provide students with practice in searching for alternatives. It deals with general values issues and life situations. For alternatives in specific situations that demand action, see Alternative-Action Search (Strategy Number 24).

PROCEDURE

The teacher may start out by saying that for many people life is just a collection of accumulated habits. This should lead to a discussion of life styles and of the importance of considering alternatives to the way we live. He then presents the students with a values issue or life problem—little or big—that may touch their lives. This is a sample list:

1. Ways to save time.

2. Things to do on a weekend in this town.

3. Ways to celebrate spring (autumn, winter, summer).

4. Creative ways to give presents.

5. Ways to earn (save) money.

6. Where to go on a date.

7. Things to do to improve race relations in our school.

The students are asked to individually brainstorm (see Strategy Number 25) as many alternatives to the problem as they can think of in the time allotted—generally from three to five minutes or a little longer, depending upon how long it takes the students to run dry.

The students are then formed into groups of three or four. Acting as a team, they are to develop a list of alternative solutions by combining their individual lists, and by adding any solutions generated in the group setting. When the groups exhaust all the alternatives they can think of within the time allotted—about ten minutes— they are to choose the three alternatives they like the best and rank order these.

The groups are then to report their results to the class as a whole. Discussion may follow. The teacher may ask if any of the students would consider using any of the new alternatives in their lives. They might agree to write Self Contracts (Strategy Number 59) at this point.

TO THE TEACHER

When students are offering alternatives, don't criticize their contributions, but do encourage them to be specific. For example, on a list of ways to save money, a student might say, "Don't buy brand names." Ask him for an example. If he says, "Buy Korvette's toothpaste instead of Crest; it's one-third cheaper and just as effective," that is a much more forceful suggestion than his previous one.

The teacher may suggest that the students write down the suggested alternatives on the following chart and check the appropriate columns. This may encourage students to consider each alternative more carefully.

ALTERNATIVE	I'LL TRY IT.	I'LL CON-SIDER IT.	I WON'T TRY IT.
1.			
2.			
3.			
4.			
5.			
6.			
ETC.			

After the brainstorming is completed, if anyone wants to hear more about a given alternative, he can ask for more information. Sometimes the person who suggested it will say, "I dunno; it just occurred to me." But sometimes he will tell the group how he or someone he knows uses the alternative, and this can be quite fascinating.

ADDITIONAL SUGGESTIONS

1. Ways to personally stop polluting our environment.

2. Ways to make new friends.

3. Ways to make learning fun.

4. Ways to get along better with our parents.

5. Ways to get the most for our dollar.

6. Ways to make a contribution to our community/ school.

7. Ways to make religion more meaningful.

8. What to do when you find yourself taking an unpopular stand on an issue.

9. Ways to make our voices heard in politics.

10. Ways of gaining more control over our own lives.

11. Ways of working more effectively in small groups.

12. Ways to settle family arguments.

13. Ways to handle the overly aggressive male/female on a date.

14. Ways to beautify our community/school.

15. How to give a great party.

16. Exciting things to do with our leisure time.

17. Ways to work for peace.

18. Ways to give the teacher some negative feedback.

19. Ways to criticize a friend about something personal.

20. Things to do and places to go on a date without spending a cent.

STRATEGY NUMBER 24

Alternative-Action Search

PURPOSE

Frequently, we find ourselves acting one way in a situation and later regretting it or wishing we had behaved differently. The clearer people are about their values, the more congruent their actions are with their feelings and beliefs and, therefore, the less often they later regret their actions.

This strategy enables students to consider alternatives for action in various specific situations. The goal is to encourage students to bring their everyday actions more consistently into harmony with their feelings and beliefs.

PROCEDURE

The teacher may introduce this activity by initiating a discussion about things that we did that we later regretted. Then the students are presented with a specific situation or vignette (see examples below) which calls for some proposed action. The teacher then asks, "Now, given all your beliefs, feelings and values related to this vignette, ideally, what would you want to do in this situation?"

Each student, individually, is to write out briefly what he would do in the given situation. Then the students break up into groups of three or four to discuss their proposals and try to decide which of their solutions would be the most desirable. They may not necessarily end up in agreement, but they should try. After ten or fifteen minutes, the discussion can move to the whole class.

SAMPLE VIGNETTES

1. You are walking behind someone. You see him take out a cigarette pack; withdraw the last cigarette; put the cigarette in his mouth; crumple the package and nonchalantly toss it over his shoulder onto the sidewalk. You are twenty-five feet behind him. Ideally, what would you do?

2. There is a boy in your class who has a body odor problem. You know the general sentiment is, "He's not such a bad kid, but I just hate to get near him." You hardly know him—you just have sort of a nodding acquaintance at a friendly distance. Ideally what would you do?

3. You are pushing a shopping cart in a supermarket and you hear a thunderous crash of cans. As you round the corner you see a two-year-old being beaten, quite severely, by his mother, apparently for pulling out the bottom can of the pyramid. Ideally, what would you do?

TO THE TEACHER

The Alternative-Action Search is an excellent activity for role playing. Members of the small group can enact the situation as described, and try out the proposed solutions to see the possible consequences.

An excellent book on the use of role playing is *Role Playing Methods in the Classroom*, by Mark Chesler and Robert Fox. (Palo Alto, California: Science Research Associates, Inc., 1966.)

Additional vignettes for the Alternative-Action Search:

1. You are on a vacation trip and are driving to the beach with your parents. You would like to go to the amusement park, but you are concerned because you have spent most of the money you had saved for your vacation earlier. Your father stops for gasoline and you get out and walk around. A lady is walking back to her car and you see her purse fall open and her wallet fall out. You walk over, pick up the wallet just as the lady gets into her car to drive away. The edges of several ten dollar bills are sticking out of the wallet. No one saw you pick it up. What would you do?

2. You have forgotten your last two dentist's appointments. The dentist was furious the last time. You have an appointment today. You look up and see it is exactly 2 P.M., which is when you're supposed to be there. It is a 20-minute walk to his office and there are no buses. What would you do?

3. You see a kid three of four years younger than you shoplifting at the local discount store. You're concerned that he'll get into serious trouble if the store detective catches him. What would you do?

4. You're driving on a two-lane road behind another car. You notice that one of his wheels is wobbling more and more. It looks as if the nuts are coming off, one by one. There's no way to pass him, because cars are coming in the other direction in a steady stream. What would you do?

5. At a picnic, there is a giant punch bowl. One of the little kids, much to everyone's horror, accidentally drops his whole plate of spaghetti into the punch. What would you do?

6. You're at another picnic. The hostess is serving the dessert. You know that she is very fussy about cleanliness, but you see that the piece of cream pie she has given your wife is infested with ants. But only her piece seems to be like that. What would you do?

7. You're taking a really lousy course at the university. You're not doing well in the course. On the day of the final exam, someone offers to sell you a copy of what he claims is the final for only $5. What would you do?

8. You've raised your son not to play with guns. Your rich uncle comes for a long-awaited visit and, of course, he brings your son a .22 rifle with lots of

ammunition. What would you do?

9. Your father has been giving you a lot of flack about how much TV you watch. One day you come home from school and the TV set isn't working. You suspect your father has done something to the set. What would you do?

10. Your family is having a discussion about abortion and you notice that your 12-year-old daughter becomes extremely upset. What would you do?

11. You are new in town and you take your car to what is supposed to be the best garage in town. You tell him you need points and plugs, and you ask, routinely, if he would save the old plugs and points so you can see them. He says, "What's the matter, don't you trust me?" What would you do?

12. You have been active in the civil rights movement. At a dinner party you attend, two guys spend a half hour matching each other with race jokes. What would you do?

13. You're late. Your dad said you had to have the car back by midnight, or it would be real trouble for you. Two blocks away from your house, you hit a dog who runs across the street. What would you do?

14. Your mother tells you that the doctor has just told her that your dad has cancer and has only two

months to live. She has decided not to tell him. What would you do?

Most of these situations have come from the real lives of the authors. Students and teachers can suggest situational dilemmas from their own lives as examples for the Alternative-Action Search.

STRATEGY NUMBER 25

Brainstorming

PURPOSE

Brainstorming is a well-known, widely used problem-solving tool. It encourages participants to use their imaginations and be creative. It helps elicit numerous solutions to any given problem, e.g., "What shall we name this product?" "What should I do in this situation?" "How can we overcome this obstacle?" In the area of values, it is very helpful in eliciting alternatives.

RULES FOR BRAINSTORMING[11]

1. No evaluation of any kind is allowed in a thinking-up session. If you judge and evaluate ideas as they are thought up, people tend to become more concerned with defending their ideas than with thinking up new and better ones. Evaluation must be ruled out.

2. Everyone is encouraged to think up as wild ideas as

---

[11]From an in-service training resource notebook for teachers of the gifted, put together by William M. Rogge.

possible. It is easier to tame down a wild idea than to pep up a bland idea. In fact, if wild ideas are not forthcoming in a brainstorming session, it is usually evidence that the individual participants are censoring their own ideas. They are thinking twice before they spout out an idea for fear that they may come up with a silly one and sound foolish.

3. Quantity is encouraged. Quantity eventually breeds quality. When a great number of ideas come pouring out in rapid succession, evaluation is generally ruled out. People are free to give their imaginations wide range, and good ideas result.

4. Everyone is encouraged to build upon or modify the ideas of others. Combining or modifying previously suggested ideas often leads to new ideas that are superior to those that sparked them.

TO THE TEACHER

Brainstorming can be used as an activity in and of itself, or it can be used in conjunction with some of the other strategies in this book. Here are some brainstorming topics—both serious and silly—that small groups in the class might work on.

1. How many ways can you think of to make this class a happier, more enjoyable place to be?

2. Your three-ton moving van, loaded with one million pipe cleaners (or balloons or chestnuts or bras-

sieres) skids off the road, and gets struck in the mud. How many ways can you think up for using your cargo to get your truck out of the mud?

3. What interesting, new subjects might we offer at our school next year?

4. Here is an object (give the group a mirror, a ruler, a wastepaper basket, etc.). Without using words show as many funny ways as you can for using this object.

5. If our school were to change its name, what should the new name be? The suggestions made for Alternative Search (Strategy Number 23) and for Alternative-Action Search (Strategy Number 24) can be used as brainstorming activities, if desired.

STRATEGY NUMBER 26

Consequences Search

PURPOSE

The evaluation of consequences is just as important as the search for alternatives, for if we choose an alternative without thinking about the consequences, we increase the risk of making a poor choice. This strategy gives students practice in searching for the consequences of various alternatives.

PROCEDURE

The Consequence-Search Strategy is used as a follow-up activity to the Alternative Search (Strategy Number 23) or the Alternative-Action Search (Strategy Number 24). Students are given, or asked to construct, a Consequences Grid, as illustrated.

CONSEQUENCES GRID

ALTERNATIVE #1:	ALTERNATIVE #2:	ALTERNATIVE #3:

At the top of the grid they are to place, in the appropriate spaces, the three most feasible solutions they developed for one of the vignettes presented in the Alternative-Action Search, or the three best ideas from the Alternatives Search. Then, for each of these three alternatives, they are to list as many possible consequences as they can think of. This may be done individually or in groups like those formed during the previous exercises. They could use the brainstorming method (Strategy Number 25) for generating consequences.

Having considered the consequences, students are then asked to reevaluate their positions. They may, individually or as a group, rerank the alternatives or decide to drop one or more of the alternatives and look for others. If the latter happens, the activity can be repeated with the newly found alternatives.

The strategy can also be used as an independent activity. Then the teacher asks the students to list at the top of the first column an action or decision they would like to make. At the top of the second and third columns they put two alternatives or variations for the actions or decisions. They then continue as previously described, listing all the consequences and reevaluating their choices.

Sometimes a student can think of only one possibility in a particular situation or for a particular problem. In such case, he can list that alternative at the top of the first column and put "Not doing alternative number 1" at the top of the second column. (Not to choose is also to make a choice; thus, there are always at least two alternatives.) He can then explore the consequences of following and not following his choice.

STRATEGY NUMBER 27

Removing Barriers to Action

PURPOSE

Often, we find that of the seven sub-processes of valuing, the ones that are least likely to have been fulfilled are those dealing with acting on one's beliefs. Students may be willing to take a stand, to prize it and be willing to publicly affirm it, to have chosen it from alternatives, freely, with knowledge of the consequences, but they may be unwilling or unable to *act* upon it because of perceived or real barriers to action. This strategy is designed to help students identify and remove barriers to action which often block and plague their values development.

PROCEDURE

The teacher asks students to write at the top of a paper some action they would like to take or decision they would like to make. It should be an action which they are having some difficulty taking or which they fear to take. Then they are to draw a line lengthwise down the middle of the paper. On the right-hand side of the paper they are to list all the perceived or real barriers, both within and outside themselves, which seem to be keeping them from acting. On the left-hand side of the paper they are to list steps they could take which might help remove or reduce each of the barriers. Finally, on the back of the paper, they are to develop a plan of action for actually removing the barriers.

This task may be done individually or in small groups, with each of the group members taking turns having the focus and receiving help from the group. The group helps in the listing of barriers to action, steps to be taken to remove or reduce the barriers, and in developing a plan of action.

STRATEGY NUMBER 28

Getting Started

PURPOSE

Many of us have grandiose plans which we often think or talk about. However, putting these plans into action sometimes seems like a tremendous task. Like the previous strategy (Removing Barriers to Action, Strategy Number 27), this exercise helps students move toward the action level of valuing. It also encourages them to start asking themselves the question, "Am I really doing what I want to do with my life?"

PROCEDURE

The teacher prepares a ditto with three columns, as shown below.

WHAT I'D LIKE TO LEARN TO DO OR BE ABLE TO DO BETTER	DATE	FIRST STEPS
1. In music:		
2. In art:		

3. In sports:		
4. In relating to people:		
5. In school politics:		
6. In studying:		
7. Socially:		
8. With my family:		
9. Open category:		

The categories are not fixed. They can come from the teacher or from the students. At home, taking several days, the students complete the first column, writing in anything they would like to learn to do, or do better, in the designated areas. In class, the teacher asks them to choose from the items they have listed any three that they really would like to get started on. They are to assign logical, realistic dates to these items. A dozen people then volunteer to read out loud the items they assigned dates to, and several members of the class react to each volunteer by saying whether or not the dates seem realistic. Then, all the students check their own dates again and proceed to list the first steps they will have to take in getting started.

The class is then divided into groups of four or five, each group member getting a turn as focus person. The focus person discusses what he listed under First Steps.

Then he asks the other members whether they have any other suggestions for first steps, and he lists any of these he cares to.

Sometimes, the teacher may prefer to have, in the first column of the ditto, only a heading without a list of designated categories. The students will simply list as many as ten things they would like to learn to do, or learn to do better, in their life. The rest of the procedure is the same.

This strategy can be used informally (without the list) among family and friends or in group settings, when someone says he would like to begin doing something but is hesitant about, or having trouble, getting started.

Another variation of this strategy is the Ready for Summer Strategy (Number 71), described later in this book.

STRATEGY NUMBER 29

Pattern Search

PURPOSE

One of the processes of valuing is building a pattern of consistent action. However, many of the things we do which involve patterns are done out of compulsion or habit, rather than out of conscious choice. This strategy is designed to help students become aware of the patterns they presently have and of their motives and reasons for doing things in a certain pattern. After completing the Pattern-Search Strategy, students may continue in their old patterns or they may develop alternative patterns; the important thing is that, whatever they do, they do it on a conscious, free-choice basis.

PROCEDURE

The teacher asks the students a question about one possible pattern in their lives. For example, "Do you go to church or temple out of compulsion, out of habit, or because you feel it is the best thing to do?" After a short discussion the teacher gives the students, or asks them to construct a Patterns Grid, as shown.

PATTERNS GRID

WHAT PROCEDURES DO YOU FOLLOW ABOUT THIS ACTIVITY?	IS IT A PATTERN?		IS IT DONE OUT OF			DO YOU PRIZE YOUR ANSWERS?		
	YES	NO	COMPUL-SION	HABIT	FREE CHOICE	YES	NO	?
1.								
2.								
3.								
4.								
5.								
6.								
Etc.								

The teacher lists activities for which people generally follow their own specific patterns. For example:

Do you follow a pattern about....

1. Getting up in the morning?

2. What you wear?

3. How you wear or comb your hair?

4. Doing your homework?

5. Kissing good night on dates?

6. Giving presents?

The students list the items on their Patterns Grid and fill in and check the appropriate boxes on the grid. They may then break into small groups and choose one of the items to discuss for ten minutes, after which they can move on to another item and another group.

TO THE TEACHER

Compulsion means *outward* compulsion, e.g., "I don't want to get up every morning at 7:00 A.M., but I have to." Habit means an unconscious pattern or inner compulsion, e.g., "I've never really thought about it. I just have always combed my hair in bangs." Free choice means conscious choice, e.g., "I like to make presents for my friends, but I buy them for my parents." Avoid philosophical arguments about free choice. The emphasis is on the feeling the student has about his pattern. Does the sense of compulsion, the sense of habit, or the sense of free choice feel strongest to him?

The Pattern Search activity may be followed by I Learned Statements (Strategy Number 15). Or students may choose a pattern they are not particularly happy with and, in small groups, do an Alternatives Search (Strategy Number 23) to see if they can come up with ideas for a more fulfilling pattern.

ADDITIONAL QUESTIONS

What is your pattern for:

1. Parking at a shopping center?

2. Using the escalator or stairs?
3. Revealing your age?
4. Eating at a restaurant? (e.g., Are you concerned with the price, or do you order what you want?)
5. Getting places on time?
6. Paying bills?
7. Making friends?
8. Ritual at the dinner table? At Thanksgiving dinner table?
9. How you brush your teeth?
10. Getting a good grade in a course you take in school?
11. Buying clothes at clearance sales?
12. Making dates?
13. Attending meetings?
14. Responding to seeing mixed racial couples?
15. What you do at a dull meeting?
16. What you dream about at night?
17. What you daydream about?
18. Taking showers or baths?
19. What time you go to bed at night and get up in the morning?
20. How you talk about other people when they are not there?
21. Counting or not counting calories?
22. Answering your phone?
23. Doing your Christmas shopping?
24. Reading the newspaper?

25. Dealing with your old clothes?

26. Doing protective maintenance on a bicycle, a motor-cycle or a car?

27. Bringing a gift when you are invited to someone's home for dinner?

28. What you serve for a company dinner?

29. Handling green stamps that you get at the grocery store or gas station?

30. Parking at a drive-in movie?

31. Buying clothes?

32. Responding when you witness someone littering?

33. Watching movies on TV?

34. Reading your mail?

35. Crying in movies?

36. Getting out of going to parties you don't really want to go to?

37. Disposing of your dirty clothes at the end of the day?

38. Buying the large, economy size of things?

39. Making long-distance phone calls?

40. Writing letters?

STRATEGY NUMBER 30

Three Characters

PURPOSE

This strategy helps the student become clearer about his/her own goals and purposes in life. By identifying with other people's achievements and characteristics, students are helped to forge their own values.

PROCEDURE

First, the teacher asks, "If you could not be yourself but you could be someone else, what is the name of the character you would most like to be?" The students are to write down on a piece of paper the name of a person chosen from real life, fiction, the news, movies, literature, cartoons, history, etc.

Then the teacher asks them to write down the name of a character "You would least like to be like," and third, "the name of a character who is most like you."

When they have listed their three characters, the students are to break up into small groups of from three to five members. They take turns sharing their lists with their group and explaining their selections.

After the students have discussed their characters, the teacher might ask values-clarifying questions like: "Were your characters males or females? Can you think of anyone whose list of characters *you* would be on? Would your list have been different three years ago? Would your best friend be able to guess the names on your list?" Etc.

TO THE TEACHER

A certain degree of trust is needed for this strategy to work well, so that students will feel comfortable sharing their characters with each other. Therefore, it would be best to let students choose and form their own groups.

Students can pass whenever they wish.

Point out to students the need for tolerance and sensitivity in this activity. People are revealing a lot about themselves through their characters. To ridicule someone's character choice is to ridicule the person himself.

STRATEGY NUMBER 31

Chairs or Dialogue with Self[12]

PURPOSE

When we are confronted with a values conflict, choice or dilemma, several voices within our heads begin operating. One voice says, "Do this," another voice says, "No, do that." Often a third or more voices offer new alternatives and new perspectives.

This strategy teaches students a useful method for clarifying the issue at stake in a values conflict. It is a helpful tool in the decision-making process. It also graphically demonstrates that values decisions are rarely easy ones, and helps students to accept and work with some of the confusion they often experience within themselves.

PROCEDURE

The teacher introduces the activity by talking a little about the notion of internal voices. He might also provide an example by describing two or more sides of a dilemma he himself faces. Then he asks students to tune in on their

---

[12]This strategy is an adaptation of a common technique in Gestalt therapy.

internal voices. Each student is to choose a conflict he has been having in which his internal voices have been carrying on a dialogue. The dialogue might be about whether to save his allowance or earnings to buy that record player, or to go to the movies with his friend. Or it might be a decision about whether or not to tell a parent or friend something important. Then each student is to write a short dialogue or script of the conversation between his internal voices.

When students have finished writing their dialogues (or trialogues), the teacher invites a volunteer to come up front and act out his dialogue. Two chairs are placed facing each other. The student is to start the dialogue in one chair and then move to the second chair to answer himself. He continues in this manner, switching chairs to talk to himself and answer himself, until he has completed his script. The teacher then encourages him to go on acting out his internal voices as long as he can or until he reaches a resolution of the conflict. A general discussion follows. The class can ask questions of either chair—similar to a Group Interview (Strategy Number 14).

Instead of calling for a volunteer to face the whole class, the teacher may choose to break the class into small groups of three to five to share and discuss their dialogues with each other.

TO THE TEACHER

Avoid playing therapist, and don't let the class's questions go in that direction, either. Focus on the conscious choices the students are confronting and the conscious pro and con feelings and reasons they express.

STRATEGY NUMBER 32

Percentage Questions

PURPOSE

The Either/Or Forced Choice (Strategy Number 5) provides students with a relatively simple index of their feelings on various pairs of alternatives. However, life in many cases is not an either/or situation, but one involving more complex decisions. This strategy introduces the concept of percentage thinking and provides students with an opportunity to examine their priorities.

PROCEDURE

The teacher reads several percentage questions, one at a time, to the class. For example:

What percentage:

1. of your allowance or earnings would you like to save for future use? What percentage *do* you save?

2. of your dates would you like to be double dates?

3. of your free time do you spend alone, with relatives, with friends?

4. of your own money do you spend on clothes, food, movies and other amusements, books or magazines, other things?

5. of your courses in school do you enjoy?

6. are you a Volkswagen and what percentage a Cadillac? What percentage a forest and what percentage a meadow? (In other words, Either/Or Forced Choices can easily be changed to Percentage Questions.)

As each percentage question is read, the students write down their own answers. The teacher then breaks the class into small groups of from three to five students and asks them to share and discuss their answers.

The entire activity may be followed by I Learned Statements (Strategy Number 15) or by a discussion of any of the questions.

ADDITIONAL PERCENTAGE QUESTIONS

What percentage of:

1. your salary would you like to give to charity?

2. your salary would you like to give to the church?

3. the letters you receive do you answer?

4. your salary or allowance do you spend on gifts?

5. the defects in your home would you reveal to a prospective buyer?

6. women should we have in the U.S. Congress?

7. the labor force should be unemployed before the government should take some action?

8. your income should be set aside in case of an emergency?

9. your time at home should be devoted to keeping the house clean?

10. your time would you like to spend with your family?

11. blacks living with whites makes for ideal integration?

12. your time do you spend working for a cause you really believe in?

13. time do you vote in school or government elections?

14. time do you spend sleeping?

15. time do you spend working?

16. your classmates would you call friends?

17. your teachers do you think really love kids?

18. your time is spent doing things you really don't want to do each day?

19. your life could you describe as being very happy?

20. your free time do you spend reading books?

21. your free time do you spend watching TV?

22. the time you spend listening to music? Do you listen without doing anything else, just listening?

23. tax monies should go toward defense spending?

24. the people you send Christmas cards to do you hope you will get one from?

25. a person's weekend should be devoted to maintenance of the house?

26. your total reading time would you like to spend on pure nonsense? On mysteries? On newspapers? On magazines?

27. your day would you like for time to do absolutely nothing?

28. the time that you drive do you drive above the speed limit?

29. the times that someone asks you if you like what they are wearing do you tell the absolute truth?

30. of an elementary schoolchild's free time do you think should be allotted to TV watching?

STRATEGY NUMBER 33

The Pie of Life

PURPOSE

This strategy is a variation of Percentage Questions (Strategy Number 32). In its simplest form, it asks us to inventory our lives—to see how we actually *do* spend our time, our money, etc. This information is needed if we hope to move from what we are getting to what we want to get out of life. The Pie of Life can also be used to raise some thought-provoking questions about how we live our lives.

PROCEDURE

The teacher draws a large circle on the board and says, "This circle represents a segment of your life. We will do several such pies. First, we will look at how you use a typical day. Divide your circle into four quarters using dotted lines. Each slice represents six hours. Now, everyone please estimate how many hours or parts of an hour you spend on each of the following areas, on a typical school day. Naturally, your answers will differ from one another. How many hours do you spend:

1. On SLEEP?

2. On SCHOOL?

3. At WORK, at a job that earns you money?

4. With FRIENDS, socializing, playing sports, etc.?

5. On HOMEWORK?

6. ALONE, playing, reading, watching TV?

7. On CHORES around the house?

8. With FAMILY, including mealtimes?

9. On MISCELLANEOUS other pastimes?

"Your estimates will not be exact, but they should add up to 24, the number of hours in everyone's day. Draw slices in your pie to represent proportionately the part of the day you spend on each category. Your pie may look something like this:

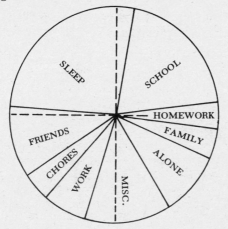

"Now think about these questions and write about them in your Values Journal. (See Strategy Number 17.)

1.   Are you satisfied with the relative sizes of your slices?

2.   Ideally, how big would you want each slice to be? Draw your ideal pie.

3.   Realistically, is there anything you can do to begin to change the size of some of your slices?

4.   Is there a Self-Contract (see Strategy Number 59) you'd be willing to make and sign your name to?"

If time permits, the students may take any one segment, for example SCHOOL, and make another pie to break down the time spent in that category. For example, the whole school pie represents five or six hours, each dotted segment an hour and a quarter or an hour and a half. The students plot a typical school day, putting in the time for each subject, for athletics, lunch, socializing, etc.

They could then take one subject area, such as mathematics, and break it down into its segments.

After each pie is executed, a series of Values-Journal questions is asked. Students should also get a chance to share their pies with one or two other students.

TO THE TEACHER

Do stress the fact that there is no right way to divide up a pie. Each of us lives a different life. There is no implication that it is necessary to change the time devoted to any specific category. The focus is on inventorying and looking at our lives more closely. Any decisions to change are up to the individual.

There are many things that can be looked at in terms of slices of the pie of life. For example: A pie on where the money goes each week, a pie on the kinds of clothes hanging in your closet, a pie on the music you listen to, or the books and magazines and newspapers you read, or the people who visit your home, etc.

In addition to being a factual inventory of your lives, the Pie of Life can ask for a subjective inventory. For example, you can plot the proportions of the day that you feel HIGH, NEUTRAL, or LOW. Or, a WORK pie can be drawn to show the portions that are CREATIVE, INTERESTING, DULL but important, and BUSY-WORK (dull and relatively unimportant).

STRATEGY NUMBER 34

Magic Box[13]

PURPOSE

To help students think about what they value.

PROCEDURE

The teacher tells students about a magic box which is very special. It is capable of making itself very small or very large. Best of all, it can contain anything that the student wants it to contain. The teacher then asks students, "If you came home from school today and found the magic box waiting for you to open, what would be in it? Remember it can have anything you want, tangible or intangible." Students are to write down their answers or tell them to the class.

The teacher might then ask other questions like:

1. What would you want in a magic box for your mother?

2. What would you want for your best friend?

---

[13]The authors learned this strategy from Jack Canfield, Center for Humanistic Education, University of Massachusetts.

3. What is the smallest thing you would want?

4. What is the largest thing?

5. What would you want for poor people?

Students are to keep what they write in their Data Banks (Strategy Number 17). After they have done this activity several times, the students might be asked to rank order (Strategy Number 4) the things they want most for themselves. They might also be asked if they have been doing anything to attain these things.

STRATEGY NUMBER 35

All About Me

PURPOSE

This strategy comes from a fourth grade teacher who asked her students to keep a notebook called, "All About Me." It provides students with an opportunity to think, and make statements, about their lives in a systematic, ongoing way. It could be considered another version of the Values Journal or Values Data Bank (Strategy Number 17), and is also similar to Pages for an Autobiography (Strategy Number 36).

PROCEDURE

The teacher has students write a story in their notebooks every other day. Stories are titled:

1. Who Am I?

2. Who Takes Care of Me?

3. I Am Proud. . . .

4. Someday I Want to Be. . . .

5.   My Funniest Experience.

6.   If I Could Change the World.

7.   My Friend.

The Unfinished Sentences (Strategy Number 37) provide many ideas for stories.

Occasionally, the students may read their stories aloud to the class, or show them to friends or to their parents. They may add to them, change them, organize them into an autobiography.

STRATEGY NUMBER 36

Pages for an Autobiography

PURPOSE

This strategy helps students develop an awareness of their life patterns through specific recall of both important and seemingly inconsequential events in their past.

PROCEDURE

The teacher explains that during the semester the students will develop pages for their autobiographies by recalling certain events from their past. (See specific suggestions below.) They will examine these experiences to see if they can detect important life patterns. Then they will judge which of these life patterns have been formed out of conscious choice and which are the result of outside pressures or of inner compulsions.

Periodically students may be formed into groups to share their autobiographical pages. The teacher can also whip around the room giving each student a chance to read part or all of a page on any given topic.

SAMPLE

1. Draw a line across the top of your paper. Mark one end Birth, and the other end with your present age. Place an X along the line for each time you changed your hair style, and write the approximate age underneath each X. Now write a story about why you changed your hair style each time; what it looked like before and after; what you thought of it at the time, and how you feel about making that change now.

2. What have you done on the New Year's Eves of your life? In one or two sentences briefly describe as many New Year's Eves as you can remember, in chronological order. What does this chronology say to you about yourself—now and in the past—and what does it show about your developing values?

3. Who have your important teachers been—not necessarily in school, but all those people, young or old, in school or out, who taught you what you regarded, then or now, as valuable lessons in your life?

4. Draw a line across the page and mark one end Birth and the other end your present age. Place an X along the line for each turning point in your life, and place your approximate age underneath each X. Now write a story describing the turning points,

how they occurred, how you felt at the time, and how you feel about them now.

5. Make a list of the best friends you have had throughout your life. Write a little about how you met, what you did together, why you liked each other, why you may have drifted apart. Who is or are your best friends now? Is your present pattern with your friends similar or different from your pattern in the past?

6. For each of the following, tell something about where you learned it and from whom:[14]

    a. How did you learn to ride a bicycle? Who helped?

    b. Who taught you how to dance? Where?

    c. When did you first learn how to jump rope?

    d. Who taught you Monopoly, or poker, or how to play chess?

    e. How did you first learn to kiss?

    f. Who taught you how to drive a car?

    g. How did you learn how to type?

    h. Where did you learn manners?

    i. Think of something else you know how to do, and record where you learned it and from whom.

---

[14]Richard Davis, Principal of English Manor Elementary School, Rockville, Maryland, suggested this particular page for an autobiography.

ADDITIONAL SUGGESTIONS

1. How many different places have you lived in your life? Tell when, where and why you moved.

2. What modes of transportation have you used during your life?

3. How did you celebrate your last five birthdays?

4. With what organizations have you been affiliated?

5. What kinds of furniture have you lived with?

6. What did you do with your summers? List as many as you can remember.

7. What collections have you made during your life?

8. What songs have been your favorites during your life?

9. Recall any serious accidents or illnesses you have had.

10. List all the churches or temples you have attended services in.

11. Recall all the Christmas presents you have given your mother in the last five to ten years.

12. Recall all the ceremonies you have taken part in.

13. Recall the last ten times you have cried. What was each about?

14. Recall all the animals you have ever had for pets.

15. Recall all the trips you have taken in the last ten years.

16. What have been the highlights of this past year? The low points?

17. Think of all the things you have wanted to be (job occupations) since you can remember.

18. What in your life made you feel the happiest? The saddest?

19. List your greatest successes in life. Your greatest failures.

20. List all the times you have thought life was hopeless and hardly worth living.

21. Mention some of the books which have touched your life deeply.

22. What were some of the phonograph records that have meant a lot to you?

23. List all the people you've been in love with.

24. Recall certain tests or examinations which are still vivid memories.

25. What were some of your close brushes with death?

26. Recall several items of clothing which were your favorites at one time or another.

STRATEGY NUMBER 37

Unfinished Sentences

PURPOSE

This strategy helps the student reveal and explore some of his attitudes, beliefs, actions, convictions, interests, aspirations, likes, dislikes, goals and purposes—in other words, his values indicators. What often emerges from this activity is a growing awareness on the part of the student of his developing values.

PROCEDURE

The teacher provides students with a list of unfinished sentences. Some examples are:

1. On Saturdays, I like to...

2. If I had 24 hours to live...

3. If I had my own car...

4. I feel best when people...

5. If I had a million dollars I would...

6. Secretly I wish...

7. My children won't have to...

Additional sentence stems are given below.

The teacher then whips around the room calling on students to complete aloud any one of the sentences with whatever comes to mind. There can be a second or third time around, if there is time and the group seems interested. Of course, students may pass. A discussion can follow, with students elaborating on their answers, or questioning other students on their answers.

VARIATIONS

1. Each student writes out all the sentences before the oral whip begins.

2. The students write out their sentences and then break into pairs or trios and discuss their finished sentences.

3. Each student completes the sentences in writing and files them away for the present. At a later date, when students have completed several lists, they take out all of their completed sentences and look for patterns. They may discuss their answers in small groups.

4. Students write out their sentences and then code their completed sentences in one or more of the following ways.

a. Place a "P" in front of those items of which you are *proud*.

b. Place a "PA" in front of those items which you would be willing to *publicly affirm*.

c. Place a "CA" in front of those items for which you *considered alternatives*.

d. Place a "TC" in front of those items which you have *thoughfully considered*, perhaps even anticipating the consequences.

e. Place a "CF" in front of those items where you feel you were able to *choose freely*.

f. Place an "A" in front of those items which you have already acted upon or are willing to *act* upon.

g. Place a "PB" in front of those items which are or will be a *pattern of behavior* in your life.

TO THE TEACHER

Unfinished sentence stems can also be used as diagnostic and feedback tools. For diagnostic purposes, use sentence stems which are likely to evoke the desired information (For example: In my neighborhood. . . ., or I need help on . . . .) For feedback purposes, use sentence stems which might evoke evaluative responses. For example, following a unit on the Civil War you might ask students to complete sentence stems like: The thing I liked best (least) in this unit. . . ., or During this unit the teacher. . . ., or I never knew that. . . .

ADDITIONAL SUGGESTIONS

1. I wish the President would. . . .
2. On vacations, I like to. . . .
3. I'd like to tell my best friend. . . .
4. Our community would be better if. . . .
5. If I had $50, I would. . . .
6. Many people don't agree with me about. . . .
7. The happiest day in my life was. . . .
8. Some people seem to want only to. . . .
9. I believe. . . .
10. If I were five years older. . . .
11. My advice to the President would be. . . .
12. If I had a gun I would. . . .
13. My favorite vacation place would be. . . .
14. When I'm alone at home, I. . . .
15. My bluest days are. . . .
16. My best friend can be counted on to. . . .
17. I am best at. . . .
18. Something unique about me is. . . .
19. People can hurt my feelings most by. . . .
20. People who wear long hair. . . .
21. Those with whom I work the closest are. . . .
22. In a group I am. . . .
23. If someone asked me to organize a new group. . . .
24. When other people are upset and hurt in a meeting, I. . . .
25. With my boss (teacher). . . .
26. The kind of person who always asks the boss for directions. . . .

27. People who seldom let me know where they stand
. . . .

28. People who agree with me make me feel. . . .

29. Strong independent people. . . .

30. When people depend upon me, I. . . .

31. I get angry when. . . .

32. I have accomplished. . . .

33. Being part of a group that has been together for a
long time. . . .

34. I get real pleasure from being part of a group when
. . . .

35. People who expect a lot from me make me feel. . . .

36. Other people are frightened most by. . . .

37. The things that amuse me most are. . . .

38. I feel warmest toward a person when. . . .

39. I like best the kind of teacher who. . . .

40. In school I do best when. . . .

41. If I feel I can't get across to another person. . . .

42. What I want most in life is. . . .

43. When someone hurts me, I. . . .

44. I often find myself. . . .

45. I have difficulty trying to deal with. . . .

46. When I see an associate (a classmate) always agree-
ing with the boss (teacher). . . .

47. When there are heated arguments in a meeting, I
. . . .

48. I am. . . .

49. People who know me well think I am. . . .

50. My boss (teacher) thinks I am. . . .

51.   People who work for (with) me think I am. . . .
52.   I used to be. . . .
53.   I want most out of school. . . .
54.   If I had it to do all over again, I would. . . .
55.   My greatest strength is. . . .
56.   I need to improve most in. . . .
57.   I am concerned most about. . . .
58.   It makes me most uncomfortable when. . . .
59.   I would consider it risky. . . .
60.   The subject I would be most reluctant to discuss here is. . . .
61.   When I enter a new group, I feel. . . .
62.   When people first meet me, they. . . .
63.   When someone does all the talking, I. . . .
64.   I feel most productive when a leader. . . .
65.   In a group, I am most afraid of. . . .
66.   I am hurt most easily when. . . .
67.   I feel loneliest in a group when. . . .
68.   I trust those who. . . .
69.   I feel closest to someone when. . . .
70.   I feel loved most when. . . .
71.   A fat person. . . .
72.   I have never liked. . . .

Unfinished Sentences for Younger Children:

1.   If I had another week of summer vacation, I would . . . .
2.   I am most creative when. . . .
3.   If I had $1, I would. . . .
4.   An important learning experience was. . . .

5. The thing that scares me most is . . . .
6. Someday I am going to . . . .
7. Some people always seem to want . . . .
8. People I like always . . . .
9. The people in my neighborhood are . . . .
10. I cry when . . . .
11. I'm afraid to . . . .
12. Something I'm really interested in is . . . .
13. I'm happy when . . . .
14. When I grow up, I want to be . . . .
15. The funniest thing I ever saw was . . . .
16. I feel most "unfaired against" when . . . .
17. The trouble with being honest (dishonest) is . . . .
18. I like people who . . . .
19. If I could introduce a bill into Congress, I would
     . . . .
20. Twenty years from now, I hope this country . . . .
21. I feel happiest of all when . . . .
22. If I saw someone shoplifting in a store, I would
     . . . .
23. Motorcycles make me . . . .
24. I'm trying to overcome my fear . . . .
25. To say what I really, really believe . . . .
26. When my family gets together . . . .
27. If I become a father or a mother, I . . . .

STRATEGY NUMBER 38

Who Comes to Your House?

PURPOSE

Value indicators are often found in our choice of friendships and associations. This strategy is designed to help students become more aware of their friendship patterns.

PROCEDURE

The teacher asks the students to draw lines down the middle of their papers. On the left-hand side of the papers, they are to list the initials of all the people they have invited to their houses for a meal in the last year. (Younger children can list those they have had over to play.) On the right side of the papers, they are to list the initials of all the people who have invited them to their houses for a meal in the past year.

Students are then to code both columns, placing the following letters or symbols next to each name or initial:

1. R if the person was a relative, F for a friend, O for other.

2. M if the person's manners bother you.

3. P if the person generally brings a present.

4. Star the names of those people whom you are really happy to see when they come over, and on the other side, those people who you think are happy to see you when you come over.

5. X if it wouldn't matter much if the person didn't come back, or if the person didn't invite you back again.

6. S or D to indicate whether their religion is the same or different from yours.

7. SR or DR to indicate whether the person is the same race or a different race from yours.

TO THE TEACHER

This activity generates a good deal of emotional involvement and should not be entered into without enough time to work through some of the issues it raises.

Give students time to reflect on their coded lists. Then a series of I Learned Statements (Strategy Number 15) or I Wonder Statements (Strategy Number 16) are good follow-ups to this activity.

STRATEGY NUMBER 39

Strength of Values[15]

PURPOSE

This strategy provides students with an opportunity to assess the strength of their feelings on issues they themselves identify.

PROCEDURE

The teacher provides students with a worksheet containing several unfinished sentences. (See below.) Students use the stems to write sentences, or paragraphs if they wish.

The worksheet may then be filed for later reference; or an optional class discussion or small group discussion might follow.

WORKSHEET

Complete the statements below. You may write one sentence or a whole paragraph. Write "nothing" for any sentence for which you have no answer, or "pass" if you'd prefer not to say.

---

[15]Developed by Fred McCarty.

1. I would be willing to die for. . . .

2. I would be willing to physically fight for. . . .

3. I would argue strongly in favor of. . . .

4. I would quietly take a position in favor of. . . .

5. I will share only with my friends my belief that. . . .

6. I prefer to keep to myself my belief that. . . .(This is for the student's private record.)

STRATEGY NUMBER 40

Strongly Agree/Strongly Disagree[16]

PURPOSE

This strategy forces the students to examine the strength of their feelings about a given series of values issues. It serves many of the same purposes as the Values Continuum (Strategy Number 8) and Spread of Opinion (Strategy Number 9), except that students are not allowed to take a middle or neutral stand.

PROCEDURE

The teacher provides students with a worksheet containing a series of belief statements. (See sample worksheet below.) Students complete the worksheet individually. Then the teacher breaks the class up into groups of three to share and discuss their responses. For at least some part of their discussion time, the trios should use the Values Focus Game (Strategy Number 18) or the Rogerian Listen-

---

[16]The authors wish to thank Dale U. Alam, Associate Professor of Education, Michigan State University, East Lansing, Michigan, for his developmental work on this strategy.

ing exercise (Strategy Number 51) to facilitate communication.

WORKSHEET

Instructions: Circle the response which most closely indicates the way you feel about each item:

> SA = Strongly Agree
> AS = Agree Somewhat
> DS = Disagree Somewhat
> SD = Strongly Disagree

Item   *Response*

1. Students are losing respect for
   teachers.   SA AS DS SD

2. People are basically good.   SA AS DS SD

3. Giving grades encourages
   meaningful learning in school.   SA AS DS SD

4. There is a life after death.   SA AS DS SD

5. I am racially prejudiced.   SA AS DS SD

6. I would encourage premarital
   sex for my son.   SA AS DS SD

7. I would encourage premarital
   sex for my daughter.   SA AS DS SD

8. I prefer police brutality to
   riots.   SA AS DS SD

9. Marijuana should be
   legalized.   SA AS DS SD

10. Familiarity breeds contempt.   SA AS DS SD

TO THE TEACHER

Students are to interpret the belief statements as they
wish. Indicate that there is no correct way to interpret
them. They are to be used simply as thought and discussion starters.

Additional belief statements may be constructed by
turning the Interview Questions (Strategy Number 12) into pro and con statements. Belief statements may also be
gleaned from student compositions, political speeches,
current issues. The students, as well as the teacher, may
make them up.

STRATEGY NUMBER 41

Taking a Stand[17]

PURPOSE

This strategy provides students with an opportunity to take a stand that they believe in on a controversial issue. It easily leads into a good discussion on that issue.

PROCEDURE

The teacher or the students select a controversial issue—something that people have strong feelings about. (Perhaps something they are currently studying.) Then each student writes a slogan about that issue on a sheet of construction paper or cardboard. The following are examples of slogans on energy and the environment:

DON'T BE A LITTERBUG!

SAVE A TREE—USE RECYCLED PAPER!

SAVE A TREE—EAT A BEAVER!

[17]The idea for this strategy comes from Dale V. Alam, Associate Professor of Education, Michigan State University, East Lansing, Michigan.

GIVE A HOOT—DON'T POLLUTE!

ENVIRONMENTALISTS ARE FOR THE BIRDS!

SAVE THE WHALES!

THERE IS NO ENERGY CRISIS!

SAVE THE REDWOODS!

PROGRESS BEFORE POLIWOGS

NO NUCLEAR PLANTS!

IF YOU NEED A JOB—
EAT AN ENVIRONMENTALIST!

RIDE A BIKE TO WORK!

Students then hold a demonstration by walking around the room carrying their signs above their heads so everyone can read them. After the demonstration, the signs are taped to the walls around the classrooms. A discussion of the issue follows.

This activity may induce students to write to their congressman or to send a letter-to-the-editor expressing their stand on the issue and the reasoning behind the stand.

If there is enough interest, the class might hold its demonstration in the cafeteria, hallway, or outside the building.

STRATEGY NUMBER 42

Values in Action

PURPOSE

This strategy focuses on the action side of valuing. It helps students see alternatives for action and asks them to find some form of action that suits them. Finally, the strategy requires students to actually engage in a planned action to bring about some desired change and then to evaluate the results of their action.

PROCEDURE

The teacher asks students to make a list of five changes they think would improve some aspect of their school, community, state or country. Or the teacher may provide the class with a list of issues and ask them to describe five changes which they would like to see made in any of these areas.

The teacher then passes out the "You Can Do Something About It" worksheet (see below) to each student. Each student completes the form by putting a check by any of the alternatives which he has ever done, and an asterisk next to any of the alternatives he would consider doing.

The teacher then asks the students to select one of their five changes and identify which types of action could be used to work toward the change they want to effect. Finally, each student is to select two types of action, and for a period of a month, actually engage in both of these actions to bring about the desired change.

A month later, the class members discuss what they did and what results, if any, occurred. (Typically, some students are successful and others are frustrated, which is a good picture of reality for students to experience.)

WORKSHEET

You Can Do Something About It!

Most of us, when we see something wrong, want to try to do something about it. Often, however, we remain inactive because we don't know what we might do. Below are some things people have done to achieve desired changes. Which of these acts is *your* way of doing something?

CAUTION: All action should be informed action; consequently, reading, learning, interviewing, discussing and generally becoming better informed are necessary first-steps before doing something.

Write a Letter

_____ 1.   Write a letter to the editor of your local newspaper. People read these columns more fre-

quently than almost any other section of the daily newspaper. You can influence public opinion.

_____ 2. Write a letter to your Congressmen or your Senators. Compliment them for something they have done about a problem you are concerned about. Washington counts those letters. They really are influenced by the mail from home.

_____ 3. Send a letter to someone in the news who has done something you respect or admire. You would be surprised how lonely it can be for someone who has made the news for doing something different.

Attend a Meeting or Organize One

_____ 1. Write one of the organizations working for a cause you believe in and ask to be put on the mailing list announcing meetings.

_____ 2. Scan the newspaper for announcements of open meetings of groups in which you are interested.

_____ 3. Ask your own club or civic group, church group, etc., to have a meeting or invite in a guest speaker on a topic you are deeply concerned with. Program chairmen are always looking for good meeting ideas. They probably will be glad to let you help.

Take Part in Some Action

_____ 1.   You can distribute leaflets from door-to-door, or at a subway entrance.

_____ 2.   Picketing may be your cup of tea; it often has an impact.

_____ 3.   Organize a petition drive. Even 20 signatures could make news or cause some public official to take notice.

_____ 4.   Interview people who are in a position to influence others. Sometimes just a series of perceptive questions can make an issue come alive.

_____ 5.   Wear a button.

_____ 6.   Take part in a peaceful march or in some other demonstration.

_____ 7.   Go as a member of a delegation to see some official on an issue.

Facts-to-Face Acts

_____ 1.   Speak up for your point of view. (For example, if someone says something derogatory about a race or a religion, talk to him about your point of view.)

_____ 2.   Try to get someone to read a pamphlet or an article which argues for a different position than the one he holds.

_____ 3. Try to close the gap between what you say and what you do. Let your life be a living argument for what you believe in.

Use the back of this sheet to list any additional ideas you have about what people can do. YOU CAN DO SOMETHING. Yes, you!

TO THE TEACHER

Does this seem like a somewhat odd assignment? Is a part of you wondering, "Do I have a right to require my students to take an action?" Many teachers react this way. It's a sad commentary on our schools, we think, when requiring students to write poetry, for example, is considered quite normal, but requiring them to fight for something they believe in is practically unheard of.

STRATEGY NUMBER 43

Letters to the Editor

PURPOSE

To make a public affirmation is one of the processes in developing values. One of the best (and cheapest) forums for public affirmation is the letters-to-the-editor page of the daily newspaper. It is democracy in action, and Tom Paine would have given his right arm for a chance at such a broad audience. Readership surveys show that the letters-to-the-editor is one of the most widely and consistently read sections of the typical newspaper.

This strategy, a variation on Values in Action (Strategy Number 42), asks students to make a public affirmation—both to the class and to the community at large. For many students, breaking into print has been a real affirmation of both the power of the pen and the right of the citizen to shape his world.

PROCEDURE

Each student writes and mails a letter to the editor of any newspaper or magazine in the country. He brings into class a carbon copy of his letter and these are tacked up on a bulletin board for the month. As the letters get printed, if they get printed, they are clipped out and taped to the carbon copy on the bulletin board. At the end of the month, students get a chance to read their letters out loud and to tell why they wrote what they did.

TO THE TEACHER

This strategy fits very well into social studies units on citizenship and into English units on writing formal letters.

STRATEGY NUMBER 44

I Urge Telegrams

PURPOSE

This strategy provides a simple means by which students can clearly state something that is important to them. Often, the expression of urgency in the classroom encourages the student to then take some action in his own life.

PROCEDURE

The teacher gives each student a 4×6 card or, better yet, a blank Western Union telegram form. He asks the students to choose a real person and write a telegram to that person beginning with these words: "I urge you to...." The message is to consist of 15 words or less (or 50 words for a night letter). The student is to sign his name to the telegram.

I Urge Telegrams can be sent to nationally known politicians in Washington, to local officials, to people in the entertainment or the sports world; or even to relatives or friends. In each case, the telegram should reflect something the sender feels is important, something he values.

Students can be called upon to read their telegrams to

the class. Sometimes a discussion will break out over some of the telegrams.

Or the telegrams may be taped to the walls and students go on a gallery walk to see what others have written.

Students can write telegrams all during the semester. Each telegram is placed in a folder (see Values Data Bank, Strategy Number 17), and when each student has written six, he spreads them out on his desk and makes I Learned Statements (Strategy Number 15) about them. Group discussion might also take place to find out whether a particular sequence seems common to many telegrams.

STRATEGY NUMBER 45

Sensitivity Modules[18]

PURPOSE

This strategy tries to bridge the gap between the world of the classroom and the world our students see on television and experience in their own lives. It provides a brief unit of experience, something the student must do that will enable him to become more sensitive to issues and people in the world around him. Such real experiences give substance to the students' developing values.

PROCEDURE

The teacher or class thinks up one or more experiences that would help the students better understand a subject they are studying. For example, here are some sensitivity modules used by suburban classes studying poverty, race, police, welfare, ghettoes, and other related issues:

---

[18]For a longer discussion of the sensitivity-module strategy, see Kirschenbaum, Howard: "Sensitivity Modules"; *Media and Methods*; January, 1970; and Simon, Sidney B.: "Sensitivity Modules: A Cure for Seniorities"; *Scholastic Teacher*, September 21, 1970. Excerpts for this section are used with permission of *Media and Methods*.

— Wear old clothes and sit in the waiting room of the State Employment Office. Listen, observe, talk to some of the people sitting next to you. Read the announcements on the bulletin board, etc.

— Attend church services some Sunday in a storefront church.

— Go to an inner-city elementary school and read a story to a child in kindergarten or first grade. Hold the child on your lap.

— Go to magistrate's court and keep a list of the kinds of cases brought before the magistrate. Who are the "customers"? How are they treated?

— Spend a few hours in a prowl car traveling with a team of policemen. Listen to the squad car radio. Ask questions. If the policemen park and walk the beat, walk with them.

— Live for three days on the amount of money a typical welfare mother receives to feed a son or daughter closest to your own age.

— Spend a morning making the rounds with a visiting nurse.

The class is given a week or two to engage in one or more of these sensitivity modules. They work in pairs. They then share their experiences with the class. The discussion which follows is invariably more informed and livelier than ever before.

TO THE TEACHER

Whites will not be overly welcome these days if they go slumming in black ghettoes, any more than blacks would be in all-white neigborhoods. This issue needs to be examined and all the realities explored before any team goes out.

All new experiences are risk-taking experiences, because we never know how they might turn out. Generally, the more the student has to do, the newer the experience for him, the greater the risk he has to take, the deeper will be the sensitivity which results from it. The more passive the student's role, the less he gets out of it. Naturally, the age of the students will be an important factor to be considered in creating sensitivity modules. There should also be an intelligent concern for students' safety. But risk cannot, and should not, be entirely eliminated, because it is central to the experience.

Sensitivity modules do not all have to be on controversial social and political issues. Here are some examples of experiences, or sensitivity modules, initiated by teachers in conjunction with regular classroom work.

1. One teacher, when the class was reading Helen Keller's *Story of My Life*, had her class walk around in school and in their homes blindfolded for a day so they might become more sensitive to Helen Keller's way of experiencing the world.

2. An elementary school teacher who was doing a unit on inventions and inventors who have changed our way of

life asked each class member to invent some useful object for his home.

3.   A math teacher tried to bridge the gap between the classroom and the outside world by asking his students to help their parents calculate the family's yearly income tax—using the long form.

4.   A history teacher had the members of his class work for political candidates of their choice during an election year as one way of studying how politics work—a realistic addition to the textbook.

5.   Some students wonder why they have to learn to write formal letters in junior high school. So some teachers ask them to write letters-to-the-editor or to Congressmen, which they actually mail. Of course, the students have to become knowledgeable about the subject they are writing on in order to express their own views.

6.   In teaching elementary children about the early world explorers, one teacher had her children go out and actually "discover" new parts of the city. One instruction was to "find a new and faster route to the ball field." The gap between the world of Columbus and their own world in the city was narrowed.

7.   One high school class studying World War II took a trip to a Veterans' Hospital where the students interviewed many of the patients.

8.   Children studying the great melting pot that is

America visited with each other's grandparents and with people in old-age homes, interviewing people who were the real, live immigrants at the beginning of this century to find out about their experiences.

A good book or movie, a trip to a museum, a guest speaker—any number of traditional teaching devices can serve as sensitivity modules—if the student is truly involved in the experience and if it is a new experience for him.

A course for high school juniors and seniors can be organized around sensitivity modules. The students are given a long list of modules, around the subject of the course, and do about one module a week. Class discussions are centered around sharing and discussing the students' experiences.

ADDITIONAL SUGGESTIONS FOR SENSITIVITY MODULES

Most of these suggested activities were designed for white suburban students. Teachers of inner-city students can easily create modules for exploring the all-white world.

1. Sit in the waiting room of the maternity ward of a city hospital whose patients are mostly charity cases. Strike up a conversation with any other person in the waiting room.

2. Hand out birth control pamphlets in an inner-city

area. (Be aware that some black people believe that birth control is a form of genocide.)

3. Compare prices and quality of a list of grocery staples at the chain store supermarket branch in your own neighborhood with the prices and quality in one of the same chain's branches in the inner-city area. Also, check the weights on five or six prepackaged meat or produce items.

4. Borrow a portable tape recorder and interview an elderly citizen who has lived in the same neighborhood for ten or more years.

5. Go to the community health center and take a seat in line. Examine the attitudes of the personnel who work in the health center. Talk to some of the patients who have come for help.

6. Read at least two issues, cover to cover, of *The Monitor*, *The Tribune*, *The Afro-African*, or another black newspaper.

7. Compare the prices of the same brands and models of record players, TV sets, and transistor radios at your local store with the prices of those on display in a credit store in the inner-city area.

8. Try to call City Hall with a complaint that your landlord did not give you heat, or has not repaired a roof leak, or that the toilet is not working. Better yet, find a neighbor with a real complaint and offer to help him get it fixed.

9. Attend a meeting of a civic group such as the Human Relations Commission, the Welfare Rights Organization, or the Neighborhood Association.

10. Go to a local candy store at a time when a local junior high school has just been dismissed. Buy a can of soda and sip it slowly while listening and observing.

11. Get on the morning train or bus that the black domestics take to get to their housekeeping jobs in the suburbs.

12. Find a school teacher who believes in making home visits, and ask if you can go along.

13. Go to the Goodwill Industries store downtown and see how many school clothes you can buy for a family of four children if you had $15 to spend.

14. Turn off the heat in your own house some nights in January or February and spend the night in a cold house.

15. See a showing of the movie, "The Jungle," made by the Oxford Street Gang.

16. Read *Manchild in the Promised Land, Go Tell It on the Mountain, The Autobiography of Malcolm X*, or some other book which tells what it is like to grow up black in America.

17. Some hot afternoon, stop into an inner-city bar for a cool drink. Anticipate the reaction a black might

get if he came into a neighborhood bar in your own neighborhood.

18. Ask to help chaperone a dance at the Youth Education and Welfare Center (YEWC), or some other community center in the neighborhood.

19. Find out which days garbage is collected in various areas of the inner-city. Compare the frequency with the garbage pickup in your own neighborhood.

20. Go to the local campaign headquarters for the Democratic and Republican parties and work a couple of hours with local people, canvassing leafleting, or making phone calls.

21. Walk four or five blocks in the inner-city at lunch hour. Buy a sandwich and a cup of coffee in a luncheonette where you are the only white person.

22. Go to an area that blacks are just beginning to move into. Survey real estate companies who have signs up. Try to find out if they have been involved in blockbusting in other areas of the neighborhood or city.

23. Work up a little lesson on something you think is important and contact a local junior high school and get permission to teach a group of children your carefully planned lesson.

24. Interview a constable on some recent evictions or

repossessions he has handled.

25. Get up early some morning and take one of the buses in the ghetto which take laborers out to pick fruit and vegetables. Ask some questions. Better yet, go along and pick.

26. Spend a weekend at a workcamp run by the American Friends Service Committee, participating in a combination of seminar and clean-up, paint-up projects.

27. Talk to a school dropout and find out what he or she thinks about how to keep kids in school.

28. Make up a large poster on rat control and ask a building superintendent if you can tack it up in the hallway of his building.

29. Tour a housing project and evaluate the toilet facilities provided for the project's 3- to 4-year-old population, particularly when the children are playing outside.

30. Take a batch of dirty clothes to a laundromat in the ghetto area. Talk to any of the other people waiting for their wash to get done.

31. Write and mail a letter to the editor of one of the city's daily newspapers on any discovery you made during your exposure to these sensitivtiy modules.

32. Write a letter to one of your congresspeople about

something you saw in any of these sensitivity modules that you think needs correction.

33. Find a middle-class black (maybe a student in one of your classes) and ask him (or her) where he is now living and about other places he has lived. Find out, also, about any experiences he has had with real estate agents.

34. Join with three other students and the four of you go to the ghetto and do a survey of people who were relocated due to luxury apartment-house building in the city.

35. Go to one of the little grocery stores in the neighborhood a week before welfare checks are distributed and note the prices of various staples. Go back on the day the checks come out and see if there are any price changes.

36. If you are a male, go get a haircut from a black barber.

37. Answer an advertisement in the newspaper for a job as a common laborer or for assembly work in a factory. Fill out the application blank and go for the interview if called.

STRATEGY NUMBER 46

Unfinished Business

PURPOSE

Inevitably as people get personally involved with one another in their search for values, they develop unfinished business—that is, they will have things they would like to talk about further but which were interrupted because of lack of time. This strategy provides students with a convenient tool to settle things which they would like to go back and discuss.

PROCEDURE

Introduce the notion of unfinished business and suggest that any time students have a free moment inside or outside of school, they might approach someone with whom they have unfinished business and say, "I have some unfinished business with you. Do you have time to talk?"

Unfinished business can also be introduced on a more formal basis by allotting a period of time each week for students to take up in class any unfinished business they have with each other or with the teacher.

Unfinished business can take the form of:

    a.   A question

b.   A compliment or some personal praise

c.   Criticism or some negative feedback

d.   The resumption of a discussion which was interrupted

e.   A statement one would like to make to someone

EXAMPLES

"I have some unfinished business with you regarding that
argument on the playground."

"I have some unfinished business with you. You did
something last week in the room which was great, and I
didn't tell you...."

"I was wondering what you meant this morning when
you said...."

TO THE TEACHER

Once students get used to the idea of Unfinished Business,
they will no longer need to use the stock phrase, "I have
some unfinished business...." They will resume their unfinished business simply by saying to the person what they
have to say. Structuring it this way at the beginning,
however, seems to legitimize the process for the students
and helps them begin confronting each other in this manner.

It is important to note that unfinished business can be
positive, negative or neutral—criticism, praise, or just an
unresolved issue, unanswered question or unfinished conversation.

STRATEGY NUMBER 47

Personal Coat of Arms[19]

PURPOSE

Some of the most important questions which will result from values-clarification activities are: "What am I doing with my life? Am I simply settling? Am I just reacting to others, or am I in control of the direction of my life? Is my life making a difference?" This activity is an enjoyable way of helping students think about these questions.

PROCEDURE

The teacher either gives the students a facsimile of the coat of arms on the following page, or has them copy this coat of arms.

The student is to answer each of the following questions by drawing, in the appropriate area on his coat of arms, a picture, design or symbol.

---

[19]Our thanks to Sr. Louise, Principal of St. Julian's School in Chicago.

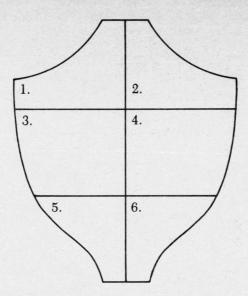

1. What do you regard as your greatest personal achievement to date?

2. What do you regard as your family's greatest achievement?

3. What is the one thing that other people can do to make you happy?

4. What do you regard as your own greatest personal failure to date?

5. What would you do if you had one year to live and were guaranteed success in whatever you attempted?

6. What three things would you most like to be said of you if you died today?

TO THE TEACHER

Students are not to use words except in area number six.

Emphasize that art-work doesn't count. The drawings can be simple, incomplete, and even unintelligible to others, as long as the student knows what they express.

Other values questions may be substituted for these; for example:

1. What is something about which you would never budge?

2. What is something you are striving to become? Or to be?

3. What one thing would you want to accomplish by the time you are 65?

4. Draw three things you are good at.

5. What is a personal motto you live by?

Students may then share, in small groups, the drawings on their coats of arms, explaining the significance of the symbols. They may cover any drawing they would rather not share.

Posting the coats of arms and holding a gallery walk is another alternative.

STRATEGY NUMBER 48

The Fallout-Shelter Problem[20]

PURPOSE

This is a simulated problem-solving exercise. It raises a host of values issues which the student must attempt to work through in a rational manner. It is often a very dramatic example of how our values differ; how hard it is to objectively determine the "best" values; and how we often have trouble listening to people whose beliefs are different from our own.

PROCEDURE

The class is divided into groups of six or seven, who then sit together. The teacher explains the situation to the groups.

"Your group are members of a department in Washington, D.C., that is in charge of experimental stations in the far outposts of civilization. Suddenly the Third World War breaks out and bombs begin dropping. Places all across the globe are being destroyed. People are heading

---

[20]The authors learned this strategy from Joe Levin.

for whatever fallout shelters are available. You receive a desperate call from one of your experimental stations, asking for help.

"It seems there are *ten* people but there is only enough space, air, food, and water in their fallout shelter for *six* people for a period of *three* months—which is how long they estimate they can safely stay down there. They realize that if they have to decide among themselves which six should go into the shelter, they are likely to become irrational and begin fighting. So they have decided to call your department, their superiors, and leave the decision to you. They will abide by your decision.

"But each of you has to quickly get ready to head down to your own fallout shelter. So all you have time for is to get superficial descriptions of the ten people. You have half-an-hour to make your decision. Then you will have to go to your own shelter.   15 MIN

"So, as a group you now have a half-hour to decide which four of the ten will have to be eliminated from the shelter. Before you begin, I want to impress upon you two important considerations. It is entirely possible that the six people you choose to stay in the shelter might be the only six people left to start the human race over again. This choice is, therefore, very important. Do not allow yourself to be swayed by pressure from the others in your group. Try to make the best choices possible. On the other hand, if you do not make a choice in a half-hour, then you are, in fact, choosing to let the ten people fight it out among themselves, with the possibility that more than four might perish. You have *exactly* one half-hour. Here is   15 MIN all you know about the ten people:

1. Bookkeeper; 31 years old

2. His wife; six months pregnant

3. Black militant; second year medical student

4. Famous historian-author; 42 years old

5. Hollywood starlet; singer; dancer

6. Biochemist

7. Rabbi; 54 years old

8. Olympic athlete; all sports

9. College coed

10. Policeman with gun (they cannot be separated)

The teacher posts or distributes copies of this list and the students begin. The teacher gives 15-, 10-, 5- and 1-minute warnings and then stops the groups exactly after a half-hour.

Each group can then share its selections with the other groups and perhaps argue a bit more, if there is time. Then the teacher asks the students to try to disregard the content of the activity and to examine the process and the values implications. He asks questions like: "How well did you listen to the others in your group?" "Did you allow yourself to be pressured into changing your mind?" "Were you so stubborn that the group couldn't reach a decision?" "Did you feel you had the right answer?" "What do your own selections say to you about your values?" These questions may be thought about or written about privately, or they may be discussed in the small groups or by the whole class.

VARIATIONS

1. Instead of eliminating four people from the shelter, students may be asked to rank order, as in a Forced Choice Ladder (Strategy Number 6), the ten candidates from the most desirable. (There is also nothing sacred about four. It could be three or five, for example.)

2. After each member of the class has ranked the ten people, they can try to come to consensus on who is to be admitted to the shelter.

3. Instead of choosing six candidates for a remote shelter, each group may be instructed to pick four out of the ten to accompany them to their own shelter.

4. Other problem situations may be invented. For example, three (or more) people need a heart transplant and will more than likely die in three weeks if it is not performed. However, only one operation can be performed. The students are to assume the role of the doctor who will perform the operation and must make the decision of who will live.

5.   The descriptions of the ten people can be changed to introduce additional values issues.

For example:

a. A 16-year-old girl of questionable IQ; a high school dropout; pregnant.

b. The same policeman with gun; thrown off the force for police brutality (or given a community-relations award).

c. A clergyman; 75 years old.

d. A 36-year-old female physician; unable to have children (or known to be a confirmed racist).

e. A 46-year-old male violinist; served seven years for pushing narcotics; has been out of jail for six months.

f. A 20-year-old male black militant; no special skills.

g. A 39-year-old former prostitute; "retired" for four years.

h. An architect; homosexual.

i. A 26-year-old male law student.

j. The law student's 25-year-old wife; spent the last nine months in a mental hospital; still heavily sedated. They refuse to be separated.

TO THE TEACHER

If one of the fallout-shelter candidates that we have provided, or that you may create yourself, gets consistently eliminated, simply give that candidate(s) more skills, or make more attractive in some way; for example, lower his age.

STRATEGY NUMBER 49

Cave-in Simulation[21]

PURPOSE

This simulation activity encourages students to think about important, and sometimes very scary, values issues: "What do I want to get out of life?" and "What do I have to contribute to my world?"

PROCEDURE

The teacher has the students sit close together in one corner of the classroom, on the floor, if possible. He turns out the lights and pulls down all the shades. He puts a lighted candle in the center of the group. Then he explains the situation.

The class, on an outing to some nearby caves, has been trapped hundreds of feet below the ground by a cave-in. There is a narrow passageway leading up and out of the cavern where they are trapped. Night is coming fast and there is no one around for miles to help. They decide they

---

[21]The authors learned this activity from Larry Krafft, Department of Psycho-Educational Processes, Temple University, Philadelphia, Pa.

will form a single file and try to work their way out of the cave. But at any moment there might be another rock slide. The ones nearest to the front of the line will have the best chances for survival. Each member of the class will give his reasons for why he should be at the head of the line. After hearing each other's reasons, they will determine the order by which they will file out.

The teacher concludes his scene-setting and instructions by saying, "So now we will go around our circle, one at a time, and each person will give his reasons for why he would like to be near the head of the line. Your reasons can be of two kinds. You can tell us what you want to live for; or what you have yet to get out of life that is important to you. Or you can talk about what you have to contribute to others in the world that would justify your being near the front of the line. Both types of reason will be considered equally; the things you want to live for can have just as much weight as the things you could do for others."

Each student gets a chance to offer his reasons. Students may pass; although in this situation, a pass means the student is deciding to allow himself to be placed near the end of the line.

TO THE TEACHER

This can be a very powerful activity. But it would only work if there is a great deal of trust in the group and they have already done quite a few values-clarifying exercises.

If it is done too soon or before the trust level is established, students will avoid seriously entering into the simulation.

STRATEGY NUMBER 50

Alligator River[22]

PURPOSE

In this strategy, students reveal some of their values by the way they react to the characters in the story. Later on, in examining their reactions to the characters, students become more aware of their own attitudes. This strategy also illustrates how difficult it is for any one teacher to say, "I have the right values for other people's children."

PROCEDURE

The teacher tells either the X-rated or the G-rated story of Alligator River (see below), depending on the age of the students. Following the story, the students are asked to privately rank the five characters from the most offensive character to the least objectionable. The character whom they find most reprehensible is first on the list; then the second most reprehensible, and so on, with the fifth being

---

[22]The authors first heard a version of this story from Rose Ann Lowe of Akron, Ohio, who attributed it to the David Frost Show.

the least objectionable.

After the students have made their own rankings, groups of four are formed in which they share their thinking and discuss all the pros and cons with one another.

Following the discussion, the teacher might ask voting questions (see Strategy Number 3) to find out how the class ranked each of the characters. (For example, "How many felt Abigail was the best character? How many felt she was the worst character?" Incidentally, this would also be a good way to form discussion groups, with those who ranked a given character first or last in the same group.)

The teacher can also ask some thought-provoking questions about the character they ranked as most offensive. For example: "Is that the kind of person *you* least want to be like?" "What kind of person would be the opposite of this character?" Write a description in your Values Journal (Strategy Number 17). List three things you could do or are now doing to be like the opposite of the person you rated as worst. Then, the teacher might ask the students to form into groups of three to share what they have written. Or a few students could volunteer to read what they wrote to the whole class.

The Alligator River Story

Rated "X":

Once upon a time there was a woman named Abigail who was in love with a man named Gregory. Gregory lived on the shore of a river. Abigail lived on the opposite shore of the river. The river which separated the two lovers was teeming with man-eating alligators. Abigail wanted to cross the river to be with Gregory. Unfortunately, the bridge had been washed out. So she went to ask Sinbad, a riverboat captain, to take her across. He said he would be glad to if she would consent to go to bed with him preceding the voyage. She promptly refused and went to a friend named Ivan to explain her plight. Ivan did not want to be involved at all in the situation. Abigail felt her only alternative was to accept Sinbad's terms. Sinbad fulfilled his promise to Abigail and delivered her into the arms of Gregory.

When she told Gregory about her amorous escapade in order to cross the river, Gregory cast her aside with disdain. Heartsick and dejected, Abigail turned to Slug with her tale of woe. Slug, feeling compassion for Abigail, sought out Gregory and beat him brutally. Abigail was overjoyed at the sight of Gregory getting his due. As the sun sets on the horizon, we hear Abigail laughing at Gregory.

Rated "G":

Once there was a girl named Abigail who was in love with a boy named Gregory. Gregory had an unfortunate mishap and broke his glasses. Abigail, being a true friend, volunteered to take them to be repaired. But the repair shop was across the river, and during a flash flood the bridge was washed away. Poor Gregory could see nothing without his glasses, so Abigail was desperate to get across the river to the repair shop. While she was standing forlornly on the bank of the river, clutching the broken glasses in her hands, a boy named Sinbad glided by in a rowboat.

She asked Sinbad if he would take her across. He agreed to on condition that while she was having the glasses repaired, she would go to a nearby store and steal a transistor radio that he had been wanting. Abigail refused to do this and went to a friend named Ivan who had a boat.

When Abigail told Ivan her problem, he said he was too busy to help her out and didn't want to be involved. Abigail, feeling that she had no other choice, returned to Sinbad and told him she would agree to his plan.

When Abigail returned the repaired glasses to Gregory, she told him what she had had to do. Gregory was appalled at what she had done and told her he never wanted to see her again.

Abigail, upset, turned to Slug with her tale of woe. Slug was so sorry for Abigail that he promised her he would get even with Gregory. They went to the school playground where Greg was playing ball and Abigail watched while Slug beat Gregory up and broke his glasses again.

TO THE TEACHER

This strategy often generates a good deal of emotional involvement. Students may attempt to attack and criticize each other's rankings. If listening to, or intolerance toward, others' ideas prove to be a problem, you can use Values-Focus Game rules (Strategy Number 18) or Rogerian Listening (Strategy Number 51).

STRATEGY NUMBER 51

Rogerian Listening[23]

PURPOSE

NEGOTIATING

Part of the ~~valuing~~ process is considering alternatives. To be open to alternatives we must be able to really listen to other people. According to Dr. Carl Rogers, good listening involves:

1. Not only hearing the words of the speaker, but hearing the feelings behind the words as well.

2. Empathizing with the speaker; that is, feeling his feelings and seeing the world through the speaker's eyes.

3. Suspending one's own value judgments so as to understand the speaker's thoughts and feelings as he himself experiences them.

STOP HERE

This strategy teaches students to really listen. Participants learn that communication is a two-way street. They

---

[23]Excerpted from Kirschenbaum, Howard, "The Listening Game," *Colloquy*, October, 1970. Reprinted with permission.

begin to understand how difficult it is really to listen to another person, especially if you disagree with him, and they come to realize how much of normal conversation is really talking *at* rather than *with* one another.

PROCEDURE

This listening exercise can be done in groups of three or more participants. One person serves as "monitor," the others as discussants. The monitor helps the discussants find a subject of mutual interest, but on which the discussants have different views or feelings. The first discussant states his position on the issue and a discussion follows.

In the typical discussion, we are so concerned with what we are going to say next, or so involved with planning our response, that we often tune out or miss the full meaning of what is being said. In this exercise, before any discussant offers his own point of view, he must summarize the essence of the previous speaker's statement, so that the previous speaker honestly feels his statement has been understood. It is the monitor's role to see that this process takes place. *Here is an example:*

FRED: . . . and what's why I'm in favor of a guaranteed, minimum annual income.

JERRY: Okay. You're saying you favor the guaranteed income because you think it will break the cycle of people staying on welfare and because it will put more money in circulation and thus create more jobs. Is that right?

FRED: You got it.

JERRY: Okay. But I think just the opposite would happen. You'd have people knowing they'd get a decent wage if they didn't work so...

FRAN: But that's ridiculous. Why would...

MONITOR: Hold it, Fran. Hold it. First of all, Jerry didn't finish his point. Second of all, you didn't restate it before responding.

FRAN: Sorry.

JERRY: Well, my point was, if somebody thinks he doesn't have to work and he'll get paid anyway, then why should he work?

FRAN: Well, I'll tell you. He'll work because...

MONITOR: Hold it, again. What did Jerry say?

FRAN: Oh, yeah. Jerry's worried this won't work. But I think...

MONITOR: Wait a minute. Jerry, are you satisfied that Fran understands your arguments?

JERRY: No.

MONITOR: Fran, do you want to try it again? Or do you want Jerry to repeat his point?

This exercise can last as long as the groups seem interested and involved in their discussions. Every now and then, the teacher asks the monitor to change roles with one of the discussants.

The exercise can be followed by I Learned Statements (Strategy Number 15) or by a discussion about listening.

TO THE TEACHER

When tempers flare, when tension rises, when parents and children, students and teachers, blacks and whites, or any group of people stop listening to one another, this listening exercise can reduce conflict and facilitate communication.

STRATEGY NUMBER 52

The Free-Choice Game[24]

PURPOSE

We frequently are in situations in which another person shares with us a choice that he is considering:

"I'm thinking about buying a new car."

"I can't decide whether to cut my hair or not."

"I have a really good job offer, but I have mixed feelings about accepting it."

"I don't know how to make up with my friend after our fight."

"I think I'd like to work for a year—you know, be on my own for a while—before going to college."

If the decision the person finally makes is to be of value to him, if it is to be a viable decision which he can be comfortable with and succeed in carrying out, it must be one that he has freely chosen himself, after thoughtful consideration of the alternatives. People who moralize,

---

[24]Excerpted from Kirschenbaum, Howard, "The Listening Game," *Colloquy*, October, 1970. Reprinted with permission. The strategy was developed in the NEXTEP Program, Southern Illinois University (Edwardsville).

grind their own ax, impose their own value judgments, plead their own causes, or justify their own lives are not the kinds of listeners who can help a person make his own choice.

This strategy teaches students a more effective way of helping others make difficult values choices. It also sharpens the students' ability to listen fully to another person.

PROCEDURE

The game can be played with three or more people in a group, but five or six in a group is usually maximally productive. One person is the focus person, one is the monitor, and the rest are the helpers.

The focus person is a volunteer who has a choice in his life that he would like to discuss with a small group of good listeners. The helpers' job is to help the focus person make his own best choice. They do this by asking questions. They may not make a statement unless they first ask permission of the focus person. Generally, their questions follow a five-step progression:

1. Understanding: They ask questions to gain enough information so they feel they have a good understanding of the focus person's choice dilemma.

2. Clarifying: They ask thought-provoking questions to test out some of their own hypotheses and to help the focus person think more deeply about his situation.

3. Exploring alternatives: They inquire about what alternatives the focus person sees open to him. With permission, they suggest other alternatives the focus person might want to consider.

4. Exploring consequences: They ask questions which cause the focus person to explore the consequences of the alternatives open to him.

5. Exploring feelings and choosing: They ask questions which encourage the focus person to explore his feelings about the alternatives and their consequences, and to think about what choice he is leaning toward at that point.

This format is not inflexible. Groups will naturally jump back and forth among the five stages of decision-making. But, in general, this structure seems to work. If the focus person first feels he is understood, he will be more open to clarifying questions. And before choosing, all the alternatives and their consequences have to be explored.

The focus person is in control. He can end the game at any time. He can and should tell the helpers if he feels pressured by their questions—if, for example, he feels they are trying to persuade him toward a given choice.

The monitor's job is to encourage the group to follow the five-step process if he senses they are putting the cart before the horse. ("I think we are exploring alternatives before fully understanding the choice situation. Focus person, are you satisfied that we understand your dilemma?") The monitor also steps in if he senses people are making statements disguised as questions, (e.g., "Don't you feel it would be wiser to...."). The game goes on for about a half-hour to forty minutes. At any point, the monitor might ask the focus person whether he feels the helpers are mostly being helpful or are trying to impose their views on him. At the end, the monitor asks the focus person if he would like to share any insights he got with the group or whether he is any closer to a choice.

TO THE TEACHER

Encourage the students to pose actual *choices* with which they are confronted, rather than *problems* they face. If the focus person raises a problem per se (lack of confidence, guilt feelings about a parental relationship, dislike of one's physical appearance) then the helpers are put in the position of being psychoanalysts, for which they are not equipped. But if the focus presents a choice situation (whether or not to ask her for a date, how much to spend on a parent's birthday present, whether or not to dye her hair) then the group can play a meaningful role.

STRATEGY NUMBERS 53 THROUGH 59[25]

NOTE *The next seven strategies (Numbers 53–59) can be treated as independent activities. However, they are most effective when treated as a seven-part exercise. This is a serious and important group of activities which focus on death, as well as life, and are, for some people, in a high-risk category. However, the impact on many students is powerful and positive.*

The entire sequence can easily take two hours. It can be done all at once or piecemeal over shorter time periods. Pencil or pen and paper are required. Silence and space for people to enjoy privacy are important.

---

[25]We have used five of these seven strategies for many years. A few years ago, we came across Phil Doster's summation of Herb Shepard's "Life Planning Project" and discovered that he, too, used many of the same strategies. We have borrowed the "Lifeline" and the "Two Ideal Days" from Dr. Shepard, as well as his ordering of the exercises. Later on, we were told that Arthur Shedlin used a similar approach many years before any of us, which illustrates how many of the strategies in this book have been in the public domain for years and, like folk songs, will continue to be passed on and adapted time and again.

STRATEGY NUMBER 53

Lifeline

PURPOSE

This simple strategy confronts students with the reality of life and death, and sets the tone for the next six strategies. It implicitly conveys the concept, "I have just so many years left and I have a choice as to how I will spend those years."

PROCEDURE

The teacher says, "Draw a horizontal line across your paper. Put a dot at each end of the line. Over the left dot, put the number zero. This dot represents your birth. Write your birthdate under this dot. The dot on your right represents your ultimate death. How long do you believe you will live? At what age do you think you'll die? Over the right dot, put a number which indicates your best guess as to how many years you will live. Write your estimated date of death under the right dot.

"Now, place a dot which represents where you are right now on the line between birth and death. Write today's date under this dot.

"This diagram is your lifeline. Look at it; study it and think about it. Let it really settle into your consciousness."

After a minute or two of meditation time, the teacher asks, "How did you feel and what did you think as you looked at your lifeline?" The teacher should encourage the students to respond freely to this question, welcoming all answers. He should not reply to the answers and he should discourage discussion, which in this case tends to stifle many students from expressing their spontaneous feelings.

TO THE TEACHER

Some students will practice avoidance reactions to this strategy. They might joke around or display some other nervous response. Try to protect those students who are really grappling with the exercise, however, by insisting on silence. Give students for whom this activity is threatening the chance to opt out, as long as they do it quietly.

STRATEGY NUMBER 54

Who Are You?

PURPOSE

This exercise calls attention to the many hats we wear in life and shows how we often allow ourselves to be defined merely by the roles we have been assigned. It also opens up alternatives to consider for the criteria by which we judge ourselves.

PROCEDURE

The teacher asks for three volunteers. They are asked to leave the room. The teacher calls in the first student and simply asks him, "Who are you?" When the student answers, the teacher asks again, "Who are you?" (Or, "And in addition, who are you?" or "Who else are you?") This process continues until the question has been asked ten times. Then, the teacher calls in the second volunteer and repeats the process.

After the third volunteer has finished, the teacher asks each student in the class to write down his own ten answers to the "Who are you?" question. (He might say, "If you had only ten words to convey who you are as a per-

son, what ten words would you use?") When the students
have all finished, the teacher calls for five or six volunteers to read their lists of words aloud.

TO THE TEACHER

Don't be embarrassed by the seeming gamery in the use of
the three volunteers. Often, fascinating variations appear
in how the three different people interpret and answer the
question. This, in turn, elicits a wider range of alternatives from each student when he is asked to list his own
ten answers.

STRATEGY NUMBER 55

Epitaph

PURPOSE

Sometimes it helps to gain perspective of life by contemplating death. What is life all about? What difference would it make if you were not alive? This strategy has us look at the meaning of our lives in a simple, but challenging way.

PROCEDURE

The teacher says, "Have any of you ever been to old graveyards and read some of the inscriptions on the tombstones? For example:

"Here lies Mary Smith. She had more love to give than was ever wanted.
"Sara Miller, A Woman of Valor.
"Ezra Jones lived as he died. Out of debt, out of sight and out of sorts.

"What would you want engraved on your own tombstones? What would be an accurate description of you

and your life in a few short words? When you have finished, I'd like to be able to call on a few of you and have
you read your epitaphs out loud to all of us."

If they wish, the students may get construction paper,
cut it in the shape of a tombstone and put their epitaph
on it, complete with stonecutter-type illustrations or deco-
rations. A very strong bulletin board display could be
made of these. Some time could be set aside for a gallery
walk in which students share with each other what was
behind the epitaphs they put on their tombstones.

TO THE TEACHER

Extend to any student the right to pass in this exercise.
Death can be frightening, and some students are supersti-
tious enough to believe that if you talk about your own
death, it will happen. Be sensitive to this.

Sometimes the students may be given time to consult
Bartlett's Quotations or old yearbooks to choose appropriate statements for their epitaphs.

It is also helpful to have an epitaph of your own ready
to read. The teacher must be willing to put his own values on the line, if he expects the students to learn to do
so. In keeping with this notion, the authors of this book
would like to share our epitaphs:

> Lee Howe: "Some men see things as they
> are and say 'why'? I dreamed
> of things that never were and
> said, 'why not'?"

Howie Kirschenbaum: "You'll know who I am by the songs that I sing."

Sid Simon: "Searcher, teacher, giver. And needing, wanting, loving and sometimes crying."

STRATEGY NUMBER 56

Obituary

PURPOSE

Again, this strategy helps the student see his life more clearly from the perspective of his imagined death. This exercise raises specific issues about the quality of one's life. It reinforces the fact that we still have a life ahead of us to do whatever we want to with.

PROCEDURE

The teacher says, "We are going to look at life by viewing it again from the perspective of death. I am going to ask you to write out your own obituary. Here is a simple format, although you are free to write your obituary in your own form. You can use as many of these suggestions as you wish, or add your own."

James Clark, age 10, died yesterday from. . . .

He was a member. . . .

He is survived by. . . .

At the time of his death he was working on becoming. . .

He will be remembered for. . . .

He will be mourned by. . . .because. . . .

The world will suffer the loss of his contributions in the areas of. . . .

He always wanted, but he never got to. . . .

The body will be. . . .

Flowers may be sent. . . .

In lieu of flowers. . . .

When everyone is finished, students may volunteer to read their obituaries out loud, or they might share their obituaries in smaller, more personal and supportive groups.

VARIATION

Students draw a line right down the middle of their papers. On the left side, they write their obituary as it would appear in the school newspaper if they were to die that day. On the right side, they write their obituary as they would like it to appear in the school or town newspaper, if they were to die three years hence.

TO THE TEACHER

Try not to generate a lot of anxiety about this exercise. Treat it matter-of-factly, but seriously. Give some comfort to the few students who will be very resistant. Let them know that this is not everyone's cup of tea; but also support those students who really get into the exercise and are trying to learn from it what it has to teach.

STRATEGY NUMBER 57

Two Ideal Days

PURPOSE

As part of the life-planning series, this strategy makes the point that we ought to be clear about what we want out of life. Students are asked to construct two perfect days, and in the process they learn more about what they really love in life.

PROCEDURE

The teacher says, "Project yourself into the future, any time from tomorrow to several years from now, and imagine two days that would be ideal for you. Imagine 48 hours of what for you would be the best possible use of that period of time. You can fantasize whatever you want; the only limit is the time limit of 48 hours.

"Write about your perfect, ideal two days. Talk about where you would be, what you would be doing, who else might be there, and so on. Try to picture what you would be doing for the full 48 hours. Go into as much detail as you can picture in your fantasy—smells, sounds, the weather, if they play a part."

After all the students have written about their two ideal days, the teacher asks for volunteers to read their stories aloud; or he divides the class into small groups in which students share their ideal days.

I Learned Statements (Strategy Number 15) may follow this exercise.

STRATEGY NUMBER 58

Life Inventory

PURPOSE

This exercise asks the student to look at some of the major themes and events of his life. In the life-planning sequence, it ties together the previous exercises and moves the student away from the fantasy level toward past and present realities.

PROCEDURE

The teacher forms students into groups of four. One person becomes the focus person, and one member of the quartet records the focus person's responses to the Life-Inventory questions. Then the focus rotates, as does the recorder. The two free members are to ask clarifying questions and help the process along.

Here are some sample questions which can be asked:

1. What was the happiest year or period in your life?

2. What things do you do well?

3. Tell about a turning point in your life.

4.   What has been the lowest point in your life?

5.   Was there an event in which you demonstrated great courage?

6.   Was there a time of heavy grief? More than one?

7.   Tell about some things you do poorly, which you have to continue doing anyway.

8.   What are some things you would like to stop doing?

9.   What are some things you would really like to get better at?

10.   Tell about some peak experience you have had.

11.   Tell about some peak experiences you would like to have.

12.   Are there some values you are struggling to establish?

13.   Tell about one missed opportunity in your life.

14.   What are some things you want to start doing now, right at this point in your life?

Fourteen questions may be too many; the teacher or class may eliminate some of these or use others. The team members must be encouraged to draw the focus person out, but not to get engaged in a discussion of the points at this time. Setting a time limit for each person helps. Ten minutes per person should be maximum. Forty minutes for the quartet.

The completed list made by the rotating recorder is handed to the focus person. This is his "Life Inventory."

If students wish, they can write out their answers first, perhaps at home, and discuss them in groups at a later time.

TO THE TEACHER

Encourage the class to avoid getting caught up in debate about any of the items brought up by a focus person. The focus person is to be drawn out in the ten minutes allotted to him and a record kept of his discoveries and disclosures during that time. The pace needs to be kept lively and fast-moving. The teacher should call time after nine minutes and get the students to move on to the next person after ten minutes.

STRATEGY NUMBER 59

Self-Contracts

PURPOSE

It is one thing to talk about wanting something in life, and another thing to do something about getting it. This strategy attempts to close the gap between what we want and what we are doing to achieve it.

This strategy can follow any values activity which generates feelings about how we live our lives. When we are seriously thinking about the quality of our lives, this is the best time for self-contracts. Thus, it is a natural conclusion to the preceding series of exercises.

PROCEDURE

The teacher says, "In this activity, you are going to make a contract with yourself about some change you would like to make in your life. It can involve starting something new, stopping something old, or changing some present aspect of your life.

"For example, perhaps you want to do something more about ecology. You might make a self-contract which says: 'For the next week, I will turn out the lights each and every time I leave my room, thus saving electricity, thus cutting down on the pollution from the electric company.' Perhaps you want to buy a guitar and will contract to save 25¢ a day until you have enough to buy your guitar. Perhaps you will contract that every time your brother teases you, you will tell him how it makes you feel and ask him to stop it, instead of simply punching him. Make the contract about any area in your life which is important to you and which you would like to work on."

The students write out their contracts and if they really intend to carry their contracts out, then they sign their name at the bottom. Volunteers may read their contracts to the class.

A week or so later, the class can take time to share and discuss how well they have been doing in carrying out their contracts.

TO THE TEACHER

You, too, should participate. Make a contract for yourself and be ready to report on your own efforts to change some aspect of your life.

One problem students often run into is that they make grandiose contracts which there is almost no hope of ever carrying out. Try to teach them to be specific and realistic, and to make contracts which can be completed.

Ready for Summer (Strategy Number 71), Getting Started (Strategy Number 28), and Removing Barriers to Action (Strategy Number 27) are all variations on self-contracts.

A comment from one of our students might help demonstrate the importance of self-contracts. "As far as self-contracts go, I usually don't like making them, but I've broken down and made one. I'm a hostess-cashier and the management is very adamant about greeting all the customers—something I never do because I feel false when I do it. However, tonight I've decided to give it a try, to see if I can become comfortable doing it through simple repetition."

STRATEGY NUMBER 60

How Would Your Life Be Different?

PURPOSE

Remember the TV programs "The Millionaire," "Superman," and "Run for Your Life?" Each of them was quite a success, and each appealed to the same basic fantasy: "How would my life be different if....?"

This strategy uses these fantasies and others to help students think more deeply about some of their hopes and aspirations, and about what they are doing to achieve them.

PROCEDURE

The teacher says to the class, "You have just been informed by your doctor that you have only one year left to live. You believe that his diagnosis is absolutely accurate. Describe how your life during the next year would be different if you were to receive this news."

After the students have had time to think and write on this question, they can share their ideas in small group or whole group discussion. After the discussion, the teacher raises the question: "If you would change your life in some way, what's stopping you from moving in that direction now?" The students can just think about this, or they can write about it or discuss it in small groups.

OTHER EXAMPLES

1. How would your life be different if someone handed you a bona fide, tax-free gift of one million dollars?

2. How would your life be different if you had the powers of Superman?

3. How would your life be different if you had a fairy godmother who could transform your appearance in whatever way you desired?

4. How would your life be different if you became President of the United States (or Dictator of the World)?

TO THE TEACHER

Help the students see the values indicators behind their fantasies. For example, a student says he'd like to be Superman so he could fly. He'd spend all his time flying, he says. You ask, "Why would you want to do that?" He says, "So I could feel free like a bird." You say, "So you value freedom?" He agrees. You bring it back to present reality by asking, "Are you doing anything now that

makes you feel free or that is working toward that goal?"
Or, "What is there in your present life that prevents you
from feeling free?"

STRATEGY NUMBER 61

What Is Important—A Song

PURPOSE

For all of us, the question, "What is important?" represents a lifelong search. This song, designed for younger children, is a useful way to encourage students to think about what they regard as important in life.

PROCEDURE

The teacher plays the simple song given below on guitar or piano, or he and the class sing it without musical accompaniment. Then they sing it again, and when they reach the line, "Tell me if you know," any student who wants to contribute something of his own which he feels is important may do so. The song continues until students run out of ideas, or the teacher senses it's enough. The song can be repeated frequently during the course of the year.

It is a good idea to get the students to record the items they contributed to the song into their Values Journals (Strategy Number 17). Data collected at different times are very useful as students look for trends in their lives.

What is im -por -tant   that's what I

want to know. What is im - por - tant

tell me if you   know.   (Music)

(music) (music) is im - por -tant   I

tell you and   it's   so.

Ask students to think of what their mothers or their fathers might say is important, or other teachers, people in
the news, or historical or literary characters. Substitute
these names for "I" in the line, "I tell·you and it's so."

STRATEGY NUMBER 62

I Am Proud—Song

PURPOSE

The I Am Proud song is used to elicit statements of prizing and cherishing. It is a musical version of the Proud Whip (see Strategy Number 11).

PROCEDURE

The class sings together, and when they come to "and I'll tell you," one student tells of something he is proud of having done. The song is repeated as often as is desirable at the time, with many or even all students getting a chance to tell something they are proud of.

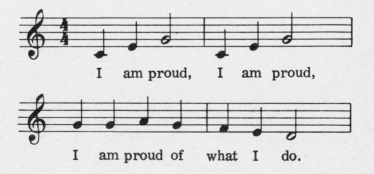

I   am proud and   I'll tell you.

Words and music by Marianne Simon, Center for Humanistic Education, University of Massachusetts.

VARIATIONS

As with the Proud Whip, the teacher can narrow the topic to one of the areas of confusion and conflict, e.g., tell about something you are proud of in relation to money, or school, or family.

The song can tell of being proud of other people by changing the words to, "...I am proud of you know who; I am proud and I'll tell you."

STRATEGY NUMBER 63

What's in Your Wallet?

PURPOSE

We can learn a lot about what we value by looking more closely at some aspects of our lives which we never thought were very important or had values implications. Looking at what we carry in our wallets, or on our person, illustrates this point.

PROCEDURE

The teacher says, "Take out three things from your wallet (or purse) that show three different things you value. These three items can be anything at all; the mere fact that you carry them in your wallet says something. Place the three items on your desk and begin thinking about what you will tell us about what any or all of them mean to you and your value system."

Whip around the room, giving each student a chance to say something about his life as evidenced by the items he carries, day in and day out, in his wallet. Follow up the exercise with some I Learned Statements (Strategy Number 15).

TO THE TEACHER

When you give the first instruction, there will be some students who will say, "I don't carry a wallet." They can choose items from their pockets or handbags or even notebooks. Or you can simply say to them, "That's OK. Let's see what the other students come up with."

Make it very clear that, as usual, anyone can pass on this exercise. They also need not feel obliged to show three items; one or two are fine, too.

This makes an interesting introductory activity with a new group. The activity can be conducted with groups of three which are selected as follows: Each student shows one thing from his wallet, handbag or notebook. Then the teacher calls on one person to choose any other person in the group in whom he is interested on the basis of what that person showed from his wallet. The second person chooses another person on the same basis, and they form a trio. Then the teacher calls on a new person to begin selecting a new trio. The trios then continue the activity as described above.

This could be one method of forming Assist Groups (Strategy Number 79).

STRATEGY NUMBER 64

Clothes and Values[28]

PURPOSE

Whether we like it or not, our clothes often tell other people something about our values. It would seem important for us to know what messages we send through the clothes we wear and to look at whether or not these are the messages we do, in fact, want to communicate. This strategy begins this process.

The exercise advances the notion that often we do something hoping that it will have one specific effect, while in reality, it has quite another effect. We don't dress completely unconsciously, although some of us work a lot harder at making a statement with our clothes than others.

PROCEDURE

The teacher gives the students, or has them draw, the following chart:

---

[28]This is adapted from an exercise the authors first learned from Jerry Weinstein, Center for Humanistic Education, University of Massachusetts.

Item of Clothing	What I *want* my clothing to say about me	What my clothing *does* say about me to others
1. Shirt or blouse		
2. Slacks, skirt, etc.		
3. Shoes		
4. Sweater, sport jacket, etc.		
5. Watch or other jewelry on wrist or hands		
6.		
7.		
8.		

In the first column the students are to list, in some detail, the clothing they are actually wearing at the time.

The teacher then says, "What we wear often tells something about our values. We often make statements with our clothes. What do you want to say about yourself with what you picked out to wear today? Examples might be, 'I want to appear very MOD.' Or, 'I want people to know I'm on the varsity team.' Or, 'I want the boys to know I have shapely legs.' Or, 'I want to convey a considered sloppiness.' Be as frank as you can and try not to be defensive as you fill in the second column. Later you will get a chance to check out with other people how they see you and what you convey to them by what you are wearing today.

"If you do not think you have anything to convey

through some aspects of your clothing, leave those spaces blank. You can still find out what you *do* convey to others by those aspects of your dress. And if several categories of dress all contribute to one effect for you, group these together in some way."

As each person completes the task, groups of three are set up, and they fill in for each other the third column. It is advisable to cover up the second column by taping a paper over it before filling in the third column. Impressions should be recorded without comment.

Then each student checks to see what, if any, are the differences between what he wanted to convey and what he actually did convey. If time permits, students can get additional feedback by forming a second trio. The whole class can discuss the topic of clothes and values, when the activity is completed.

TO THE TEACHER

Remind the class that feedback from only two other students cannot be considered a fair sample of the way everyone views the way we dress.

This exercise can be repeated at different times in a semester. Each student should save his papers (Values Data Bank, Strategy Number 17) to look later for patterns in his habits of dress and to gain further insights about his values.

There are other things that can be surveyed in the same way. For example: List six prominent things in your room at home. What do you *want* them to say about you when someone enters your room. What do these six things *actually* say about you to people who have been in your room? Or: What are five things you have written on the covers of your school books? What do you want them to say about you? What *do* they say to other people?

STRATEGY NUMBER 65

What We Know
and What We Want to Know

PURPOSE

This strategy helps show the relationship between the standard subject matter of the school curriculum and the values level of subject matter as discussed in chapter one. It argues that what would be most helpful to students about any topic they study in school is how that topic can illuminate their own search for values. This strategy is also a good way to generate student interest in a particular topic.

The activity teaches a pattern of learning that can be useful throughout life, when students are trying to find answers to their real questions—their values questions.

PROCEDURE

At the beginning of a unit of study, for example, a unit on Lung Cancer, the teacher says, "There are many things you probably already know about this topic, even though we may not have studied it formally in school. Let's see what you do know about lung cancer."

Two students are picked to be board secretaries to record items of information on the chalkboard. No judgment is made about any item. If a student contributes it, it goes up on the board. (Later on, either the class will discover or the teacher can point out any factual errors.)

When all the things the group knows about lung cancer are up on the chalkboard, the teacher says, "OK. Now, what don't you know about lung cancer that you would like to know? Let's organize another list of all the things we want to find out about this topic."

Again, the board secretaries record all of the ideas. If the students trust the process, they often come up with important personal values-issues about the topic. For example: "What are the odds on my getting lung cancer?" or, "How can I get my father to quit smoking?"

The class looks at the "What We Want to Know" items, and organizes them into logical clusters. These clusters become the basis for group reports or for individual research.

TO THE TEACHER

Before the group brainstorming, it might help to take some time to ask people to make their own lists of things they know and things they would like to know about the topic.

Naturally, the teacher can and should contribute items to both lists.

This strategy can be useful with topics as far-ranging as

a contemporary issue like "race relations" and a historic issue like "The Boston Tea Party," or a scientific issue like "The Digestive System." Generally, it is most helpful when it looks at an issue that has some relevance to human behavior. If you try to use this strategy with a unit on "The Major Products of Argentina," you may discover that there is little or nothing the students want to know about that subject.

If you have trouble organizing ideas to form research committees, here is one way to do it. Ask the class to look for any two topics on the list that seem to go together. Assign each of them the Roman numeral I. Then find two other topics which also seem to mesh under a different heading; give them Roman numeral II. Go down the list, and classify each item. Some will form new categories and get new Roman numerals, and some items will fit into the already assigned Roman numerals. When this task is completed, committees can be organized around each of the Roman numeral topics.

STRATEGY NUMBER 66

The Miracle Workers[29]

PURPOSE

This strategy poses a problem that confronts the student with many attractive alternatives to choose from. It helps him get in touch with his feelings about what is important to him.

PROCEDURE

The teacher provides students with the worksheet below containing the names of fifteen miracle workers. Each student works alone and chooses the five miracle workers he values the highest; that is, the five whose gifts the student would most like to receive. Then, each student is asked to pick five more names. This leaves five miracle workers in the least desirable group.

Then students form into groups of three to discuss their choices and see if they can discover any patterns. Some helpful questions are: "What seems to link together the

---

[29]Developed by, and used with the permission of, Mark Phillips, Center for Humanistic Education, University of Massachusetts.

five most desirable people and what joins the five least desirable to you?" "What values were you upholding in your choices?" "Are there any choices that somehow seem out of place with the others in that grouping?"

At this point, the discussion can take different forms. Some teachers invite students to share their feelings about a miracle worker in their most or least desirable group. Or the class can role play the miracle workers, with each person arguing for why he is more powerful, more needed, more useful for mankind than the others.

Then the teacher asks the students a difficult question: "What are you now doing to achieve what your top five miracle workers could do for you? Make a list, in your Values Journal (Strategy Number 17), of what you are doing or could do."

Finally, the teacher asks for some self-contracts (Strategy Number 59) based on the learnings from this exercise. The implication is that each of us is a miracle worker. What miracles do we want to strive for? Where do we begin? How can we help each other?

WORKSHEET

A group of 15 experts, considered miracle workers by those who used their services, have agreed to provide these services for the members of this class. Their extraordinary skills are guaranteed to be 100% effective. It is up to you to decide which of these people can best provide you with what you want.

The experts are:

1. *Dr. Dorian Grey*—A noted plastic surgeon, he can make you look exactly as you want to look by means of a new painless technique. (He also uses hormones to alter body structures and size!) Your ideal physical appearance can be a reality.

2. *Baron VonBarrons*—A college-placement and job-placement expert. The college or job of your choice, in the location of your choice, will be yours!

3. *Jedediah Methuselah*—Guarantees you long life (to the age of 200) with your aging process slowed down proportionately. For example, at the age of 60 you will look and feel like 20.

4. *Drs. Masters Johnson and Fanny Hill*—Experts in the area of sexual relations, they guarantee that you will be the perfect male or female, will enjoy sex and will bring pleasure to others.

5. *Dr. Yin Yang*—An organismic expert, she will provide you with perfect health and protection from physical injury throughout your life.

6. *Dr. Knot Not Ginott*—An expert in dealing with parents, he guarantees that you will never have any problems with your parents again. They will accept your values and your behavior. You will be free from control and badgering.

7. *Stu Denpower*—An expert on authority, he will make sure that you are never again bothered by authorities. His services will make you immune from all control which you consider unfair by the school, the police, and the government (the armed forces included!).

8. *"Pop" Larity*—He guarantees that you will have the friends you want now and in the future. You will find it easy to approach those you like and they will find you easily approachable.

9. *Dr. Samantha Smart*—She will develop your common sense and your intelligence to a level in excess of 150 I.Q. It will remain at this level through your entire lifetime.

10. *Rocky Fellah*—Wealth will be yours, with guaranteed schemes for earning millions within weeks.

11. *Dwight D. DeGawl*—This world-famed leadership expert will train you quickly. You will be listened to, looked up to, and respected by those around you.

12. *Dr. Otto Carengy*—You will be well-liked by all and will never be lonely. A life filled with love will be yours.

13. *Dr. Claire Voyant*—All of your questions about the future will be answered, continually, through the training of this soothsayer.

14. *Dr. Hinnah Self*—Guarantees that you will have self-knowledge, self-liking, self-respect, and self-confidence. True self-assurance will be yours.

15. *Prof. Val U. Clear*—With her help, you will always know what you want, and you will be completely clear on all the muddy issues of these confused days.

TO THE TEACHER

Even though there may be a great deal of noise and joking during this discussion, it is more than likely to be deadly serious. Don't be put off by the noise and bombast. Underneath, students will be trying very hard to make some sense out of the lives they lead.

Some good follow-up exercises could be the Values Survey (Strategy Number 7). The game format of the Miracle Workers makes it a good first experience of the three; it is somewhat more involving and less threatening than the other two strategies.

STRATEGY NUMBER 67

Ways to Live

PURPOSE

This strategy asks students to formulate their own philosophy of life by responding to 13 other ways to live. It leads to the consideration of alternative life styles, and causes students to more thoroughly consider their own life styles.

PROCEDURE

The teacher passes out copies of the worksheet, Ways To Live. (See below.) When students have responded to the 13 ways to live, they are to rank order all 13, from their first preference to their last.

The teacher has the students choose partners. Each pair discusses one or two ways to live to which they had quite different reactions. They spend five minutes discussing their differences and trying to understand the other person's point of view. Then each one finds a new partner and repeats the discussion procedure. This may be repeated several times.

Then, each student writes out his own way-to-live statement, reflecting his own philosophy of life at this point in his life. Students can borrow phrases or sentences from any of the 13 described here, or they can create their own wording and ideas.

Finally, students are asked to think of ten things they have done in the last week that are consistent with the philosophy of life or the way to live they have just described. This bridges the gap between a general philosophical statement and the way we actually live.

I Wonder Statements (Strategy Number 16) are a good conclusion to this thought-provoking exercise.

WORKSHEET

Ways to Live[30]

Instructions: Below are described 13 ways to live which various persons, at various times, have advocated and followed.

You are to write numbers in the margin to indicate how much you yourself like or dislike each of these ways to live. Do them in order, one after the other.

Remember that it is not a question of what kind of life you now lead, or the kind of life you think it prudent to live in our society, or the kind of life you think would be good for other persons, but simply the kind of life you personally would like to live.

Use the following scale, and write one of these numbers

---

[30] Reproduced with permission of author. Questionnaire from *Varieties of Human Value* by Charles Morris, University of Chicago Press, 1956. pp. 15–19.

in the margin alongside each of the ways to live:

    7.   I like it *very much*

    6.   I like it *quite a lot*

    5.   I like it *slightly*

    4.   I am *indifferent* to it

    3.   I dislike it *slightly*

    2.   I dislike it *quite* a lot

    1.   I dislike it *very much*

WAY 1: In this design for living the individual actively participates in the social life of his community, not primarily to change it but to understand, appreciate, and preserve the best that man has attained. In this life style, excessive desires are avoided and moderation is sought. One wants the good things of life, but in an orderly way. Life is to have clarity, balance, refinement, control. Vulgarity, great enthusiasm, irrational behavior, impatience, indulgence are to be avoided. Friendship is to be esteemed, but not easy intimacy with many people. Life is marked by discipline, intelligibility, good manners, predictability. Social changes are to be made slowly and carefully, so that what has been achieved in human culture is not lost. The individual is active physically and socially, but not in a hectic or radical way. Restraint and intelligence should give order to an active life.

WAY 2: In this way of life, the individual for the most part goes it alone, assuring himself of privacy in living quarters, having much time to himself, attempting to control his own life. Emphasis is on self-sufficiency, reflection and meditation, knowledge of oneself. Intimate associations and relationships with social groups are to be avoided, as are the physical manipulation of objects and attempts at control of the physical environment. One should aim to simplify one's external life, to moderate desires which depend upon physical and social forces outside of oneself. One concentrates on refinement, clarification, and self-direction. Not much is to be gained by living outwardly. One must avoid dependence upon persons or things; the center of life should be found within oneself.

WAY 3: This way of life makes central the sympathetic concern for other persons. Affection is the main thing in life, affection that is free from all traces of the imposition of oneself upon others, or of using others for one's own purposes. Greed in possessions, emphasis on sexual passion, striving for power over persons and things, excessive emphasis upon intellect, and undue concern for oneself are to be avoided. These things hinder the sympathetic love among persons which alone gives significance to life. Aggressiveness blocks receptivity to the forces which foster genuine personal growth. One should purify oneself, restrain one's self-assertiveness, and become receptive, appreciative, and helpful in relating to other persons.

WAY 4: Life is something to be enjoyed—sensuously enjoyed, enjoyed with relish and abandonment. The aim in life should not be to control the course of the world or to change society or the lives of others, but to be open and receptive to things and persons, and to delight in them. Life is a festival, not a workshop or a school for moral discipline. To let oneself go, to let things and persons affect oneself, is more important than to do—or to do good. Such enjoyment requires that one be self-centered enough to be keenly aware of what is happening within in order to be free for new happiness. One should avoid entanglements, should not be too dependent on particular people or things, should not be self-sacrificing; one should be alone a lot, should have time for meditation and awareness of oneself. Both solitude and sociability are necessary for the goood life.

WAY 5: This way of life stresses the social group rather than the individual. A person should not focus on himself, withdraw from people, be aloof and self-centered. Rather he should merge himself with a social group, enjoy cooperation and companionship, join with others in resolute activity for the realization of common goals. Persons are social, and persons are active; life should merge energetic group activity and cooperative group enjoyment. Meditation, restraint, concern for one's self-sufficiency, abstract intellectuality, solitude, stress on one's possessions all cut the roots which bind persons together. One should live outwardly with gusto, enjoying the good things of life, working with others to secure the things which make possible a pleasant and energetic social life. Those who oppose this ideal are not to be dealt with too tenderly. Life can't be too fastidious.

WAY 6: This philosophy sees life as dynamic and the individual as an active participant. Life continuously tends to stagnate, to become comfortable, to become sicklied o'er with the pale cast of thought. Against these tendencies, a person must stress the need for constant activity—physical action, adventure, the realistic solution of specific problems as they appear, the improvement of techniques for controlling the world and society. Man's future depends primarily on what he does, not on what he feels or on his speculations. New problems constantly arise and always will arise. Improvements must always be made if man is to progress. We can't just follow the past or dream of what the future might be. We have to work resolutely and continually if control is to be gained over the forces which threaten us. Man should rely on technical advances made possible by scientific knowledge. He should find his goal in the solution of his problems. The good is the enemy of the better.

WAY 7: This philosophy says that we should at various times and in various ways accept something from all other paths of life, but give no one our exclusive allegiance. At one moment one way may be more appropriate; at another moment another is the most appropriate. Life should contain enjoyment and action and contemplation in about equal amounts. When any one way is carried to extremes, we lose something important for our life. So we must cultivate flexibility; admit diversity in ourselves; accept the tension which this diversity produces; find a place for detachment in the midst of enjoyment and activity. The goal of life is found in the dynamic integration of enjoyment, action, and contemplation, and in the dynamic interaction of the various paths of life. One should use all of them in building a life, and not one alone.

WAY 8: Enjoyment should be the keynote of life. Not the hectic search for intense and exciting pleasures, but the enjoyment of the simple and easily obtainable pleasures; the pleasures of just existing, of savoring food, of comfortable surroundings, of talking with friends, of rest and relaxation. A home that is warm and comfortable, chairs and a bed that are soft, a kitchen well stocked with food, a door open to friends—this is the place to live. Body at ease, relaxed, calm in its movements, not hurried, breath slow and easy, a willingness to nod and to rest, gratitude to the world that feeds the body—so should it be. Driving ambition and the fanaticism of ascetic ideals are the signs of discontented people who have lost the capacity to float in the stream of simple, carefree, wholesome enjoyment.

WAY 9: Receptivity should be the keynote of life. The good things of life come of their own accord, and come unsought. They cannot be found by resolute action. They cannot be found in the indulgence of the sensuous desires of the body. They cannot be gathered by participation in the turmoil of social life. They cannot be given to others by attempts to be helpful. They cannot be garnered by hard thinking. Rather do they come unsought when the bars of the self are down. When the self has ceased to make demands and waits in quiet receptivity, it becomes open to the powers which nourish it and work through it; sustained by these powers, it knows joy and peace. Sitting alone under the trees and the sky, open to nature's voices, calm and receptive, then can wisdom from without enter within.

WAY 10: Self-control should be the keynote of life. Not the easy self-control which retreats from the world, but the vigilant, stern, manly control of a self which lives in the world, and knows the strength of the world and the limits of human power. The good life is rationally directed and firmly pursues high ideals. It is not bent by the seductive voices of comfort and desire. It does not expect social Utopias. It is distrustful of final victories. Too much should not be expected. Yet one can with vigilance hold firm the reins of self, control unruly impulses, understand one's place in the world, guide one's actions by reason, maintain self-reliant independence. And in this way, though he finally perish, man can keep his human dignity and respect, and die with cosmic good manners.

WAY 11: The contemplative life is the good life. The external world is no fit habitat for man. It is too big, too cold, too pressing. It is the life turned inward that is rewarding. The rich internal world of ideals, of sensitive feelings, of reverie, of self-knowledge is man's true home.

By the cultivation of the self within, man becomes human. Only then does there arise deep sympathy with all that lives, an understanding of the suffering inherent in life, a realization of the futility of aggressive action, the attainment of contemplative joy. Conceit then falls away and austerity is dissolved. In giving up the world, one finds the larger and finer sea of the inner self.

WAY 12: The use of the body's energy is the secret of a rewarding life. The hands need material to make into something; lumber and stone for building, food to harvest, clay to mold. The muscles are alive to joy only in action: in climbing, running, skiing and the like. Life finds its zest in overcoming, dominating, conquering some obstacle. It is the active deed which is satisfying; the deed that meets the challenge of the present, the daring and the adventuresome deed. Not in cautious foresight, not in relaxed ease does life attain completion. Outward energetic action, the excitement of power in the tangible present—this is the way to live.

WAY 13: A person should let himself be used. Used by other persons in their growth, used by the great objective purposes in the universe which silently and irresistibly achieve their goal. For persons' and the world's purposes are basically dependable and can be trusted. One should be humble, constant, faithful, uninsistent. Grateful for affection and protection, but undemanding. Close to persons and to nature, and willing to be second. Nourishing the good by devotion. One should be a serene, confident, quiet vessel and instrument of the great dependable powers which move to fulfill themselves.

STRATEGY NUMBER 68

Christmas Gift Giving

PURPOSE

The Christmas season gives us a good opportunity to look at our patterns of gift giving. This strategy has us consider a unique alternative to our regular gift-giving pattern. However, this strategy could really be done at any time during the year.

PROCEDURE

The teacher tells the students to divide their papers into five columns. The instructions are: "In the first column, list ten people who are very close to you. They can be family, friends, co-workers, etc.; but they ought to be ten people who touch your life frequently and with intensity.

"In the second column, write the gift you gave that person last Christmas, or the gift you plan on giving this Christmas. If you didn't give him a Christmas gift, recall a gift you gave that person at another time during the year. If you haven't given that person any tangible gift in the last couple of years, just leave the space blank.

"In the third column, list a gift you could give to each person that would dramatically change some aspect of that person's behavior. Perhaps it would be the gift of 'Being able to listen better,' or 'Learning to laugh at the funny tricks life plays on you.' Give each of these people a gift which you think would make him happier, as well as changing his behavior.

"In the fourth column, try to list some tangible gift you could give each person that would help him achieve the behavior change you listed in the third column. Take some time to think about this.

"Finally, in the last column, list a gift that each of these people could give *you* to change one or more of *your* behavior patterns. Try to imagine what behavioral change each of the people you listed would like to endow you with. More than one person can give you the same gift. If you think you would get the same gift from all ten, it tells you something important."

The follow-up takes place in small groups or Assist Groups (Strategy Number 79). The groups discuss action plans for actually bringing about some of the changes the members both gave and received as gifts through this exercise. For example, the group may try to find a present that will help someone listen better.

Another form this exercise could take is to have class members give each other a series of "values presents" at Christmas time. For example, "I give Geraldine more confidence in publicly affirming what she believes." Or,

"My gift to Tom would be the ability to hit low curve balls."

STRATEGY NUMBER 69

Past Christmas Inventory

PURPOSE

Christmas, like birthdays, comes every year. Some of our students can look forward to 50 to 70 or more Christmas. This exercise looks at Christmas card giving and can help make future Christmases more consistent with our values.

PROCEDURE

In January, the teacher brings in the Christmas cards he received that Christmas. He has sorted them out into several categories and explains his sorting:

"Pile one is the stack of cards from people to whom I also sent a card.

"Pile two is from the people who sent me a card, and to whom I had not originally sent a card, but *did* send one after I received theirs.

"Pile three is from people who sent me cards, but to whom I did not send cards.

"Now, I also have one list of names of people to whom I sent a card, and who did not send me one. A second list of people who sent me a card, but I suspect did so only after receiving one from me.

"I would like each of you to please prepare a similar inventory."

When this has been done, the class is divided into groups of three. Using Focus Game rules (Strategy Number 18), each member gets five minutes to talk about his Christmas card giving pattern.

The whole class then discusses the issue of Christmas card giving in general. Finally, the students could make Self-Contracts (Strategy Number 59) about what they want to do about Christmas cards next Christmas.

This exercise could also be combined with an Alternative Search, (Strategy Number 23) on "Alternatives to the Store-Bought Christmas Card."

TO THE TEACHER

Some students may object to examining Christmas card lists from a values viewpoint. They may feel that not everything should be subject to examination. This is a good chance to reaffirm the seven processes of valuing (see chapter one).

Students should have the chance not to inventory if they wish, but they shouldn't interfere with those students who do want to find out more about their patterns in this way.

STRATEGY NUMBER 70

RDA's.
Resent-Demand-Appreciate[31]

PURPOSE

Many of the conflicts we have with people close to us are values conflicts. It often boils down to the fact that we just see life differently. What you like, I don't like. What I want, you don't seem to want as much. A lot of these values conflicts generate strong feelings of resentment. This exercise attempts to teach students how to handle feelings of resentment which grow out of values conflicts. The students learn to make what we call RDA's.

PROCEDURE

The teacher asks students to fold a paper into four long, vertical columns, and says, "In the first column list the ten people with whom you come into closest contact, day after day. You would probably list your parents, your boss, your girlfriend or boyfriend, your best buddy, your teacher, etc. You can list more than ten or less than ten if

---

[31]Based on a technique learned from Janet Lederman.

you want to.

"In the second column, for at least three of the people on your list write a sentence (or two) which expresses a resentment you have about some behavior trait they have. Don't be frightened by the word 'resentment.' It's a real word and one which our feelings understand well enough.

"Begin your statements with the phrase, 'I resent you.' For example: 'I resent you, Jim, for not doing your share of the work around the house,' or, 'I resent you, Doris, when you apple polish our Spanish teacher.'"

After the students have written their three resent statements, the teacher asks them to think about this idea: "Behind every resentment we feel for someone else, there is an implied demand we really want to make. We rarely have resentment by itself. There is something we want changed, and we want it changed fast, usually.

"In the third column, try to write down the demand you really have for each of the I Resent Statements you made. Make it specific and realistic. For example, 'I resent you, Jim, for not doing your share of work around the house, and I demand that you take out the garbage on Tuesday nights and that you shovel the driveway when it snows.'

"The fourth column is for the 'A' part of RDA. It means 'appreciate.' Our resentments and demands would actually mean more to the person we offer them to if we tried to see things from his point of view and appreciated why he behaves as he does. For example, 'I resent you, Jim, for not doing your share of work around the house, and I demand that you take out the garbage on Tuesday nights and that you shovel the driveway when it snows; but I do appreciate the fact that you are involved with so many things around school that you sometimes don't have time, and sometimes are so caught up in your other activities that you don't remember.'

"Or, 'I resent you, Doris, for apple polishing our Spanish teacher, and I demand that you regain your integrity and treat her with your honest feelings; but I appreciate the amazing skill you have of blatantly buttering her up without arousing the least suspicion in her.'"

The students should now write I Demand and I Appreciate statements for the three people for whom they originally made I Resent statements.

TO THE TEACHER

You will note that in our examples, there have been two kinds of appreciate statements. One kind conveys empathy and lets the resented person know that you appreciate his side of the story, too. The other type of appreciation conveys an admiration for some aspect of the resented behavior. For example, "I resent it when you tell off-color jokes at parties, and I demand that you cut it out, but I appreciate that you are a good story teller and the jokes *are* pretty funny."

Some teachers may be fearful of what will happen when they begin to allow resentments to come out in class. But the resentments are there anyhow, interfering with the climate you are trying to build. Only by allowing them—yes, even encouraging them—to surface can they be dealt with. Dealing with strong feelings is an important part of the value-clarifying process, and we need every possible communication skill we can develop to express these feelings at an honest level for close examination. Classes that learn to use RDA's (and it must be stressed that all three parts are essential) seem to grow tremendously in their capacity to relate to and grapple with real values issues.

The teacher encourages the students to use RDA's as a regular part of class discourse. Thus in the midst of a discussion, a student might say, "I resent you, Susie and Barry, for laughing at what I just said, and I demand that when I'm being honest like this you don't laugh at me; but I appreciate that it probably did sound funny to you. Only that didn't make it hurt any less."

VARIATION

Each student writes out RDA's for three other students in the class. The whole class then forms a circle. Each person in the circle, in turn, reads one of his resent statements aloud. Then you go around the circle again and each student adds his demand statement to his original resent statement. The third time around have each student make all three statements—resent, demand and appreciate. If necessary, the teacher can make a rule that no one student may have more than three statements directed at him. Thus, students can't gang up on a scapegoat.

If the words *resent* and *demand* are too strong for the occasion, students may substitute other words which better describe their feelings. For example, "It *bothers* me, Bob, when you use that expression. I *wish* you'd find a different way to say what you want to. I appreciate that you probably weren't even aware that it bothered me."

The demand need not call for a specific behavior change. It can go something like, "I demand we take some time to talk over the situation and work something out."

STRATEGY NUMBER 71

Ready for Summer

PURPOSE

Summers are often menacing to people. They provide a long stretch of time, we often think, in which we can accomplish an amazing amount of work or learning or playing. Frequently, we become frustrated because we're not having as much fun as we think we should or are not getting as much work done as we think we should. Setting realistic "shoulds" is part of values clarification. Another part of the process, important for most people, is establishing some balance between fun and productivity. This exercise brings into focus the issue of realistic planning and apportioning of free time.

PROCEDURE

The teacher says, "Summer is just around the corner and most of us have high hopes for a happy and fulfilling couple of months. We're going to think about different ways people use summers.

"Divide your paper into five columns headed by Roman numerals I through V.

"Under Roman numeral I, list all the places you'd like to go to this summer that you think would be fun. List beaches, mountains, towns, cities, you'd like to visit. Make note of the people you like whom you will want to visit. You might also mention concert halls, stadiums, theaters, etc. List all the places you really want to go.

"Then, under Roman numeral II, list all the less-than-fun things you have to, or want to, get done. Do you have a house to paint? Dead trees to cut up into firewood? An 'incomplete' to work off by doing a term paper? This category is for all the things you want to or have to get done, but which are not primarily fun.

"Under Roman numeral III, list all the books you want to get read this summer. Maybe there won't be any; but if you have been thinking of some, list them by title or by author.

"Under Roman numeral IV, list anything you want to learn to do or get better at doing. List the skills that you plan to set aside some time for developing and improving.

"Finally, under V, put down anything you want to make or produce, or have to show for the summer. It may be money, a painting, an article of clothing, an object or possession, a suntan. If you don't have anything to list, leave this topic blank.

"When you have completed your lists, choose up to ten items—no more than two from any category—that you *really* want to do this summer; things that are high on your list of priorities. Put a star next to each of these.

"For each of these starred items, answer the following questions:

1. What will I need in order to do it (e.g., money, pencil and paper, etc.)?

2. Is there anyone who can help me do it?

3. What are the first steps I will have to take?

4. What deadlines or schedule can I realistically set and stick to?"

Then, students break up into small groups and each one gets the focus for five minutes or more, to tell about his summer ahead—his plans, his goals and how he will try to get as much out of the summer as possible.

TO THE TEACHER

Sometimes students resist inventories like this one. No one should be forced to do any of these exercises. Interestingly, we have found that often the student who resists such an exercise is the student who has been very rigid and compulsive and is now trying to be more flexible and spontaneous. Thoreau is frequently a model for such students; but they tend to forget Thoreau's delight in inventorying.

STRATEGY NUMBER 72

Are You Someone Who?

PURPOSE

This strategy causes students to consider more thoughtfully what they value, what they want out of life, and what type of persons they want to become.

PROCEDURE

Students will answer "Yes," "No," or "Maybe" for each item. This is done by circling either Y, N, or M—symbols which appear before each question.

After students have answered all the questions, each student reads to the class one question which he answered with an emphatic "yes" or "no" and tells why he answered that way.

Finally, the students make their own lists of twenty "I Am Someone Who..." sentences. They may use ten of the items from the given list. Then they make up ten new items, expressing personal goals and hopes they have for the future, or values or behaviors they follow in the present.

THE QUESTIONS

Are you someone who...

Y   N   M   1.   is likely to have six or more children?

Y   N   M   2.   will probably never give up smoking?

Y   N   M   3.   will most likely become a PTA president?

Y   N   M   4.   will insist upon having wall-to-wall carpeting?

Y   N   M   5.   will be the first one in the class to get to Europe?

Y   N   M   6.   will never want to go to Europe?

Y   N   M   7.   will probably wear long hair all of your life?

Y   N   M   8.   is likely to practice natural childbirth?

Y   N   M   9.   is likely to marry someone of another religion?

Y   N   M   10.   is likely to grow a beard some summer? (boys)
is likely to date a boy with a beard? (girls)

Y   N   M   11.   will most likely never grow a beard?
(boys)
will never date a boy with a beard?
(girls)

Y   N   M   12.   will always read the sports page?

Y   N   M   13.   will always read the comics?

Y   N   M   14.   will be a consistent writer of letters
to the editor?

Y   N   M   15.   will marry for money?

Y   N   M   16.   will run for public office?

Y   N   M   17.   would be a difficult person to be
married to?

Y   N   M   18.   would not consider getting engaged
without a ring?

Y   N   M   19.   is likely to publish a short story
someday?

Y   N   M   20.   is likely to play the lead in an ama-
teur theatre group?

Y   N   M   21.   is likely to get fat?

Y   N   M   22.   will watch a lot of TV at age 40?

Y   N   M   23.   will insist on going to a restaurant at
least twice a week?

Y   N   M   24.   will probably allow your male children to grow long hair?

Y   N   M   25.   will not permit your hair to gray naturally?

Y   N   M   26.   is apt to go out of your way to have a black (white) as a neighbor?

Y   N   M   27.   would consider joining the John Birch Society?

Y   N   M   28.   is apt to become increasingly active in civil rights?

Y   N   M   29.   would have no difficulty if a black (white) moved into your neighborhood?

Are you someone who . . .

Y   N   M   30.   will subscribe to *Playboy* magazine?

Y   N   M   31.   will never go out without shined shoes?

Y   N   M   32.   will probably make a bad first marriage?

Y   N   M   33.   will change your religion?

Y   N   M   34.   is sure to move away from your hometown?

Y   N   M   35.   will make a career in the military?

Y   N   M   36.   will probably live to a ripe old age?

Y   N   M   37.   will refuse to live in a housing development?

Y   N   M   38.   is apt to get into trouble with the
law?

Y   N   M   39.   is likely to turn out to be a liberal
who went conservative?

Y   N   M   40.   will never hire a cleaning person?

Y   N   M   41.   may develop a drinking problem?

Y   N   M   42.   will be likely to win a Nobel Peace
Prize?

Y   N   M   43.   locks all doors and windows when
you are alone in the house?

Y   N   M   44.   can't resist a bakery?

Y   N   M   45.   has a Beatle picture in your room?

Y   N   M   46.   buys Bach records out of your allowance?

Y   N   M   47.   is apt to experiment with pot?

Y   N   M   48.   orders ginger ale rather than a cock-
tail when out on a date?

Y   N   M   49.   never wears seat belts?

Y   N   M   50.   always uses seat belts?

Are you someone who...

Y   N   M   51.   would get therapy on your own ini-
tiative?

Y   N   M   52.   has insomnia?

Y   N   M   53.   is apt to do anonymous favors for
people?

Y   N   M   54.   cheats on exams?

Y   N   M   55.   brown-noses teachers?

Y   N   M   56.   would lend your last subway token?

Y   N   M   57.   is a thoughtful lover?

Y   N   M   58.   would lie to save someone else's rep-
utation?

Y   N   M   59.   wakes up often with nightmares?

Y   N   M   60.   could be satisfied without a college
degree?

Y   N   M   61.   knows nothing about birth control?

Y   N   M   62.   will make a nervous mother? father?

Y   N   M   63.   will make a faithless husband? wife?

Y   N   M   64.   will drive too fast?

Y   N   M   65.   can't have fun at a party unless
slightly drunk?

Y   N   M   66.   will pin or be pinned four or five times?

Y   N   M   67.   would be a great teacher of very young children?

Y   N   M   68.   is very materialistic?

Y   N   M   69.   is a talking liberal who hasn't done anything?

Y   N   M   70.   will make a wonderful father? mother?

Y   N   M   71.   will never want much money?

Y   N   M   72.   will never have as much money as you want?

Y   N   M   73.   will change your hair color several times in your life?

Are you someone who . . .

Y   N   M   74.   will never go to a beauty parlor?

Y   N   M   75.   will insist on a small wedding?

Y   N   M   76.   is indifferent to food?

Y   N   M   77.   will put sport jackets and ties on your three-year-old son?

Y   N   M   78.   turns the radio on the minute you get into the bedroom?

Y   N   M   79.   can't quit the late show in the mid-
                      dle?

Y   N   M   80.   never buys a sex paperback?

I Wonder Statements (Strategy Number 16) can follow
this exercise.

STRATEGY NUMBER 73

Who's to Blame?

PURPOSE

We often get insight into our own lives by taking sides in someone else's conflict. This little story has much the same purpose as Alligator River (Strategy Number 50) and the Fallout-Shelter Problem (Strategy Number 48). It gets the discussant to see what he is protecting in his own value structure.

PROCEDURE

The teacher says: "Here is a story in which you will meet several characters. You will be asked to rank order them, with the person most distasteful to you in the number one spot and the person least distasteful to you in the number four spot. Here is the story:

"There is a high school student who is selling marijuana (pot) to junior high school kids because he desperately needs money to get the transmission fixed on his car. He needs the car to get to his job as a busboy at the country club. The car he bought, it turns out, had its transmission filled with sawdust, which kept it running just long enough to get beyond the ten-day guarantee given to him by the used car salesman. When confronted, the used car salesman said, 'Look, that's just the way we took the car in. We didn't check it. We didn't do anything to it, good or bad. Go see the guy who sold it to me.'

"The man who sold the car to the used car dealer sold it in a hurry, because he bought a new house in the sub- urbs and he had to raise the money for the closing costs quickly or his family would have been without a roof over its head. The car he sold was really their second car, and he was going to get around to getting the transmission fixed after they moved and got settled in their new house. But when the closing costs came due, he filled the trans- mission with sawdust and sold the car to the dealer for the wholesale book price. The used-car dealer cleaned the car up a bit, and sold it to the high school student at the retail book price, making about $85 on the deal.

"The new house buyer said he wouldn't have done what he did if he hadn't been desperate, and he blamed the banker for not telling him well in advance what the closing costs would be.

"The banker said, 'Now, if he hadn't been so cheap, he would have hired a lawyer who knows all about closing costs, but he wanted to save a few bucks and do it him- self. We handle too many deals here to be able to keep up with each individual who comes in for a mortgage. Any- how, he ought to have known that there are always clos- ing costs. But what can you expect from those kind of people? As soon as blacks begin moving into their neigh- borhoods, they rush out here to the suburbs like the plague was after them and they don't stop to think about details like closing costs and mortgage fees and so on. Well, business is business, and we're in the business of lending money, we're not lawyers for people who don't know about closing costs.'

"This is the situation. Now your job is to rank order these people. Put the one you consider least blameless in the number four spot, and the one you blame the most in the number one spot. When you have done this, we'll break up into quartets to discuss your rankings.'

TO THE TEACHER

There are many options for handling the discussion which will develop from this problem:

1. The class can role play each character being confronted by some super-conscience, and play out the arguments, pro and con.

2. If possible, get four students, each of whom thinks a different person is the least blameless, to argue his side, with the rest of the class listening in.

3. An important follow-up activity is to give students journal-writing time (see Strategy Number 17) to inventory the values, beliefs or feelings they were protecting as evidenced by the rankings they did. In effect, the teacher asks, "What do your rankings say to you about your values?"

4. The teacher can also ask students to share situations

similar to the one in the story that they may know of or may have been in.

A small warning. Never let the discussion get into a win-lose confrontation. There really is no right answer. The major reason for discussing such problem situations is to become clearer on what we seem to value.

STRATEGY NUMBER 74

Brand Names

PURPOSE

One of the functions of value-clarification procedures is to bring to a conscious level the choices we make. Often we allow ourselves to fall into patterns of choosing without ever really examining them. This strategy asks students to look at their own pattern and at their family's pattern of buying to see how many of the valuing processes went into each choice.

PROCEDURE

A ditto is distributed to the students:

ALL THE BRAND NAMES IN OUR MEDICINE CABINET	I	II	III
1.			
2.			
3.			
4.			
5.			

ALL THE BRAND NAMES IN OUR MEDICINE CABINET	I	II	III
6.			
7.			
8.			
9.			
10			
Etc.			

ALL THE BRAND NAMES IN OUR CANNED GOODS CABINET	I	II	III
1.			
2.			
3.			
4.			
5.			
6.			
7.			
8.			
9.			
10.			
Etc.			

ALL THE BRAND NAMES IN OUR GARAGE	I	II	III
1.			
2.			
3.			
4.			
5.			
6.			
7.			
8.			
9.			
10			
Etc.			

The students take the ditto home and list all the brand names they find in these three places. They are to list every brand name, not just the well-known brand names. They then continue working with the ditto in class.

In Column I the student writes the name of the person who most likely chose that particular brand. How did it get into the house? Who brought it in?

In Column II the student tells why that particular brand was chosen. He starts with the items that he himself introduced into the house, and tries to identify who or what influenced him to buy that particular brand. "Was it a recommendation from a friend? Did a salesman sell it to you? Did you buy it because you saw it advertised? Where? Write in Column II, as best you can, who or what motivated you to buy that particular brand. When you get home tonight, ask other people in your family, the ones who bought or introduced each brand into your home, what made them choose that particular brand. Try to find some explanation for each item on your list, and place it in Column II."

The next day the teacher and the class work on Column III. A check goes in Column III if the item was picked by making use of these three criteria: It was chosen after examining several alternatives. It was chosen after thoughtfully considering the pros and cons of the alternatives. It was a free choice, not a pressured one.

The discussion can then examine how vulnerable we all are to the mass media and to the pitchman's magic.

TO THE TEACHER

Don't let students get defensive or feel guilty that so many of their purchases seem to indicate that they are extremely guillible to the Madison Avenue hustler. The truth is, we are all vulnerable; but we can be less so if we begin to use the values criteria when we buy.

Younger children can learn a lot by doing a brand name survey of all their toys. They will learn that television has done an incredible job of getting them to want the latest Barbie Doll costume, the newest Hot Wheels car, etc.

Older students can examine the brand names of books

or records they have bought and the labels of clothes in their closets.

A fourth column can be added. In this column, students would write one of the following code letters:

K = I'll keep it or keep buying it.

E = I'll eliminate it or stop buying it.

C = I'll change to another brand name.

T = I'll have to think more about whether I'll keep it, or eliminate it, or change to another brand name.

A good follow-up for this strategy is Baker's Dozen (Strategy Number 75).

STRATEGY NUMBER 75

Baker's Dozen

PURPOSE

A theme which runs all through these strategies is that in order to make some sense out of the bewildering array of alternatives in our life, we have to set some priorities. This strategy gets at that issue in a fresh way.

PROCEDURE

The teacher says: "Make a list of 13 things (a baker's dozen) that you personally use around your house which make use of electricity. This includes anything at all with plugs which you, yourself, use fairly frequently.

"Now, draw a line through the three things you could live without the easiest. If, for example, there was an acute power shortage, and every home was asked to cut down on its use of electricity which three could you give up most easily? These are the three you'd cross out.

"On the other hand, which three do you find very precious? Draw circles around these items. These would be the last ones you would want to give up."

The teacher then asks for volunteers to read their circled and crossed-out items. Also, the class can make I Learned Statements (Strategy Number 15) about these 13 possessions, or about their material possessions in general.

TO THE TEACHER

Make sure that you share your own list during the discussion and let your students know where you stand on the use of appliances. If you are an ecology fan, be careful not to do excessive moralizing. Let the data speak for each person and to each person in its own way.

Instead of, or in addition to, electrical appliances, students could list 13 phonograph records they own, identify the three most- and the three least-important items. Or they could list 13 items of clothing in their closets, or 13 articles in their bedroom. In each case they choose the three they could most easily give up and the three they regard as most valuable.

The teacher can play "devil's advocate" and suggest that everyone should give the three items they crossed out to needy individuals or families. A lively discussion should follow.

STRATEGY NUMBER 76

Reaction Statements

PURPOSE

This strategy causes students to thoughtfully consider a variety of values issues and to publicly affirm their reactions to these issues.

PROCEDURE

The teacher writes a fairly short but thought-provoking statement on a large piece of newsprint or oak tag and tapes it to the wall of the room in a visible location. (Sample "reaction statements" are given below.)

The statement stays there for a week or so, with no special attention called to it. Each day, the students inevitably see the statement during the course of their other work. If the statement is a provocative one, students will think about it. They might even discuss it with their friends outside class.

Finally, whenever the teacher deems it auspicious, he asks if anyone would like to come to the front of the room and comment upon the reaction statement. Volunteers may come up, one at a time, and make a comment. There should be no debating or answering of previous comments.

SAMPLE

1. Adults get paid for their work. Kids should get paid for going to school. How about 25¢ an hour?

2. Thou shalt not kill, except in wars.

3. "Most men lead lives of quiet desperation." Thoreau.

4. If a father catches his son smoking marijuana he should turn the boy over to the civil authorities so he can be helped.

5. There were over 56,000 deaths in auto accidents last year on U.S. highways.

6. Women are really the stronger sex.

7. Students should be allowed to use curse words in the school newspaper if this will help them make a point.

TO THE TEACHER

Instead of the comments without discussion, a teacher can set aside time for a discussion of the reaction statement, if the group seems interested.

Students can comment upon the reaction statements in their Values Journal or Values Data Bank (Strategy Number 17).

Students should be encouraged to bring in reaction statements of their own and to write them out and post them.

STRATEGY NUMBER 77

Diaries

PURPOSE

Perhaps *the* best place to find the data for values-clarification activities is in the students' own lives. Diaries is a strategy that enables the students to bring an enormous amount of information about themselves into class to be examined and discussed.

PROCEDURE

The teacher or class chooses one of the Diaries. (See examples of diary topics below.)

For a whole week, or longer, students (and the teacher) keep their own individual diaries. If they have chosen a Religion Diary, they record all thoughts, conversation, and actions having to do with religion. If it is a Budget Diary they are keeping, they accurately record all income and expenditures they made that week. In a Disagreements Diary, they would record the basic facts about any disagreements they found themselves in that week—whether or not they voiced their disagreement at the time. They could also record disagreements between other people which they witnessed.

A week or more later, students bring their diaries into class. First, in groups of three, each student gets five minutes as the focus person to talk about his diary. He shares entries, tells of surprises or insights, etc.

Then the teacher asks the class a series of values-clarifying questions related to that particular diary.

For example, for the Disagreements Diary:

1. On what percentage of the disagreements did you voice your disagreement?

2. In how many of the disagreements did you find yourself actually angry?

3. What is your pattern of handling disagreements?

4. In watching other people's disagreements, did you see any examples of ways of handling conflict that you'd like to employ in your own life?

Or for the Budget Diary:

1. Which expenditures brought you a good deal of pleasure? Which proved disappointing?

2. How many expenditures did you make alone? For how many were other people present? Do you spend more easily when you're by yourself or with others?

3. How many expenditures would you label free choices?

4. Knowing what you know now, what, if anything, do you wish you had done differently about your income or expenditures?

This activity can end here, or it can be followed with I Learned Statements (Strategy Number 15), or Self-Contracts (Strategy Number 59).

SAMPLE DIARIES

1. Time Diary (how the 24 hours of each day are spent).

2. Budget Diary.

3. Politics Diary.

4. Religion Diary.

5. Independence Diary.

6. Male-Female Roles Diary.

7. Disagreements Diary.

8. Compliments Diary.

9. High Points Diary.

10. Affectionate and Tender Feelings Diary.

11. Hostility and Anger Diary.

12. Low Points Diary.

13. Decisions Diary.

14.   Doubts Diary.

15.   Any of the areas of confusion and conflict discussed
      in chapter one can become the subject of a diary.

TO THE TEACHER

Diaries are most effective, and done most conscientiously,
only when we want to keep them. Be careful in giving a
diary assignment. Be sure it ties in with something the
class is interested in, or that it grows out of a lively discussion or pertinent topic.

STRATEGY NUMBER 78

The Suitcase Strategy

PURPOSE

To have students assess the relative value of their personal possessions.

PROCEDURE

The teacher asks students to pretend that they are going on a very long voyage across the ocean to a new land. After briefly describing what students may expect to find upon arriving in the new land (see examples below), teacher explains that each student can take only one large suitcase. "We are going to be very crowded on the boat going over; therefore, there will be room for only one large suitcase each. Anything you cannot put in the suitcase will have to be left behind. Now, take out a sheet of paper and make a list of the things you will want to take."

When students have completed their lists, a few students can be called upon to read their lists to the rest of the class and give their reasons for the choices they made. A general class discussion follows.

Or the students form small groups of four or five to share and discuss their lists.

Or the teacher has students post their lists on the walls around the classroom. Students can look at each other's lists, discuss them, ask questions, and make changes in their own lists if they wish.

Students can save their lists in the Values Data Bank (Strategy Number 17). Then, after repeating the strategy several weeks or months later, students take out their lists and examine them for changes.

TO THE TEACHER

The kind of information provided students about the new land they are going to will influence their decisions about what to pack. For instance, survival items become more of a consideration in an unsettled or underdeveloped area than in a land of plenty.

Here are some sample descriptions of the new land:

This land is largely agricultural. There are a few small towns, but most of the people live and work on farms. The climate is very similar to that in the northeastern U.S. The countryside is beautiful, with many mountains and lakes.

This land is very poor and primitive, but it has been strongly influenced by its former British rulers, and it is very formal in its dress and customs. The climate is tropical all year round. Most of the people live in grass huts, but the ruling class live luxuriously and the hotels have first-class facilities.

This is a bustling, cosmopolitan resort center. People come here for their holidays from all over the world. Anything and everything is available at a price.

STRATEGY NUMBER 79

Assist Groups or Support Groups

PURPOSE

This is not a values-clarification strategy in and of itself. It is, rather, a way of organizing the class for maximum benefit in executing some of the values-clarification strategies. Many of the activities suggested in this book call for breaking up the class into small groupings. For a strategy to be most effective, the environment must be a supportive one in which students feel comfortable enough to be honest and to share their thoughts, feelings, doubts, goals and experiences with one another. Assist Groups or Support Groups should provide this trusting atmosphere when the activity is to be done in small groupings.

PROCEDURE

After several introductory, low-risk strategies have been done with the class as a whole, the teacher selects a strategy that requires working in small groups. The first few such activities should be relatively simple, non-threatening ones, such as Interview Chain (Strategy Number 13),

Brainstorming (Strategy Number 25), the Fallout-Shelter Problem (Strategy Number 48)

The teacher explains to the class that they will be working in small groups and that it is important that the group members trust one another and are good listeners. He also explains that it is better not to work with old friends, but rather try to build a listening, trusting climate with other people as well.

The class is then divided into groups to engage in the selected strategy. With primary children the teacher may choose the groupings by random selection. With older students it is usually best to give them some choice in the selection process. Ask each student to write down the names of five people in the class whom they don't know too well, but with whom they might like to work. The teacher collects the lists and works out the groupings, trying to follow the students' choices.

Another method for forming small groups is suggested in What's in Your Wallet? (Strategy Number 63).

From time to time, the teacher asks the Assist Groups to examine their own process; that is, to discuss how well they are listening to one another, whether they feel comfortable with each other, whether there are members who tend to stifle self-disclosure by making "killer" statements, how they deal with the time limits, etc.

TO THE TEACHER

Do not expect instant results with Assist Groups. It takes time for a level of trust to be built. Gradually the Assist

Groups will become more and more helpful to their members.

Avoid overusing Assist Groups. It is important that the students work with others outside their Support Groups and have opportunities to apply their learnings from the Support Groups to other group situations. Thus, when a strategy needs small groupings, sometimes the teacher may ask the class to break into their Assist Groups, and at other times new groupings will be formed.

Index of Strategies